Human Capital Management

Human Capital Management

Leveraging Your Workforce for a Competitive Advantage

Mark P. Salsbury

This is a production of

 SALSBURY HUMAN CAPITAL MANAGEMENT, LLC

To my wife Patty with love, who has always believed in me, encouraged me to do what was unordinary and uncomfortable, but adventurous and rewarding.

To my children Samantha and Michael, who along with your mom, have been and continue to be the inspiration and joy in my life. Choose your own path and be true to yourself in all your pursuits.

Contents

Preface

Like many of you, I've read a large number of business books over the years. Some of them were quite helpful to me as I sought to learn and improve as a manager. A great example is Jack Welsh's book, *"Jack: Straight From the Gut."* I liked Jack's book because he gave personal insights about his management style, supported by inspiring ideas and stories about managing at GE. Other good business books focus on collecting stories and lessons learned from well-managed and/or financially successful companies. A great example is *"Good to Great"* by Jim Collins.

The most common type of business literature I've come across over the course of my career has been the theoretical approach, rich in research data, and in support of the author's model that he/she is attempting to pitch. In my opinion, where they sometimes fall short is applying their theory or model practically.

You might be asking yourself what's different about this book? What can I offer that you haven't already heard?

"Human Capital Management: Leveraging Your Workforce for a Competitive Advantage" presents a practical business model I believe can be beneficial to small, medium or large-scale organizations, both for profit or not-for-profit.

My model is based on the concept of *"human capital management"* as a practice, and focuses on how to successfully implement organizational goals heavily reliant on the collective efforts of the people in an organization.

I've developed this model through my own experiences and expertise as a global business executive and HR leader. As such, the personal stories and anecdotes in the pages that follow are primarily taken from my own corporate experience. These experiences are based on both successes and failures. As you know, there's much to learn from success stories and failures. In fact, sometimes it's easier to see wisdom in failure than it is in success.

This book is practical, and from a business executive's point of view. It provides specific recommendations for any organization wishing to transform its human capital into a competitive advantage. I've included real-life examples to support the principles and key learning points.

This book isn't intended to deliver a new theory on culture change or change management, nor is it about how to motivate people. There are plenty of books, articles, and seminars on these topics.

This book is about the practice of Human Capital Management, and the assertion that most people-centered organizational initiatives need to be comprehensive and systematic in order for them to take root and be leveraged as a competitive advantage.

This view of Human Capital Management underscores the importance of aligning and integrating certain key organizational elements to effectively drive human capital within an organization. I refer to this approach as the Human Capital Management System.

I wrote this book primarily for people who are in a position to directly and significantly influence an organization through its human capital, that is, CEOs, HR managers, and other leaders who are charged with the responsibility to make their organizations successful. This book is also relevant for aspiring managers, professionals, and students who can learn new organizational and management techniques that will be helpful to them as they navigate their careers.

In Section 1 of this book I've laid out a preliminary view of Human Capital Management, which serves as the foundation for the chapters to follow. In this first section, the definition of Human Capital Management will be reviewed, with a description of the basic conditions and requirements necessary for organizations to transition to Human Capital Management. Next, I'll cover the increased significance Human Capital Management can have as a competitive advantage in today's business world.

In Section 2, the first piece of the Human Capital Management System is reviewed. I call this the "business foundation." In this section, we'll look at the parts that make up the business foundation, and how they need to be aligned for maximum benefit to occur. Companies that effectively align the business foundation are well positioned to drive human capital.

Section 3 addresses the Human Capital Management Wheel or what I like to call the "performance wheel." This section provides an overview of the performance wheel itself and the identification of key organizational components or spokes within the performance wheel. Each of these spokes will be covered individually in separate chapters to elaborate on them appropriately.

Section 4 delves into the leadership characteristics required for Human Capital Management to be successful. This section emphasizes the CEO and Human Resource roles in the implementation of Human Capital Management. While it's important for other senior members of management to be capable and committed to this transformation, with the exception of the CEO's role, I believe none is more crucial to the success of Human Capital Management than the role of HR.

This book is intended to offer a practical roadmap to mobilize the human capital talent in your team, organization or company. Whether you're an executive looking to navigate an organizational culture change or an aspiring leader looking to learn new skills in Human Capital Management, it's my sincerest wish that this book is of value to you.

Forward & Endorsements

*Opening Remarks by **James Salsbury**, Business Consultant specializing in Operations Management and full-time faculty member of Bentley University's McCallum School of Business, former CEO of Whidden Memorial Hospital in Everett, Massachusetts and Deaconess Waltham Hospital in Waltham, Massachusetts:*

"Throughout my career as a business executive and educator, I've met scores of consultants and read hundreds of business books and articles, including this book, *Human Capital Management: Leveraging Your Workforce for a Competitive Advantage.* That's why, when my brother Mark asked me to preview his book, I was curious to see if he had something to offer that was different. After all, so many of the business books I've read are steeped in theory, weak on practice or full of interesting stories, but lacking in direction.

Upon reading it, I'm happy to report that this book is a valuable tool in providing a practical and useful roadmap for business leaders and human resource executives to follow in achieving their strategic objectives through the most difficult advantage for competitors to duplicate, the organization's workforce.

As pleased as I am to endorse this book, I'm even more enthusiastic about Mark's capability to guide organizations through Human Capital Management implementation. His senior level management capabilities in blending vision/strategy with operational execution are a hallmark of his career.

But don't just take my word that this book is a valuable management tool for people-centered organizations.

Here's what others have to say:"

"A *must* read for CEOs, Sr. Management teams, and HR Practitioners. Mark brings to life the synchronization of Strategy, Structure, and Execution in a pragmatic and insightful manner. *'Human Capital Management: Leveraging Your Workforce for a Competitive Advantage'* combines the insight and experiences of a global executive with a systematic approach to transformational change strategies designed to embed executable human resource tactics into an organization's performance. I would highly recommend this book to global organizations as a competitive advantage in aligning their organization for results!"

Keith Chrzanowski
Senior Vice President, Human Resources
Given Imaging Ltd.
Duluth, Georgia

"With his book, Mark brings his years of valuable experience in people management into defining a practical system that many companies can easily implement. A system that will enable them to obtain the best performance and achieve their strategic objectives, from their most important asset: their people.

It was exciting to read how Mark very effectively captured, through real operational examples, the evolution of the system he defines. This includes some of the ideas we shared as colleagues early in our careers, ideas that won't be alien to most senior managers, as well as those with less experience. I found his book captivating and easy to read, and will share this book with my staff and the rest of my organization."

Armagan Akar
President & CEO
Teseda
Portland, Oregon

"Unlike many other academic books that preach theory, in *'Human Capital Management,'* Mark Salsbury gives CEOs and HR leaders practical solutions on how to utilize an organization's most important asset: its people. This book is easy to follow and understand with great real-world examples to support the principles and concepts offered. Mark's writing reflects his own leadership and management style, combining strategic thinking and operational execution that's crucial for executive success in today's global business environment. One or the other is not enough, you need to have both.

I would highly recommend this book to business leaders in any industry, public or private sector, and particularly to those in the HR community. Whether you're a seasoned HR leader or upcoming professional, by following the steps outlined in this book, you'll have a roadmap to chart a course for your organization, from a proven contemporary."

R. Campbell Fitch
Global Human Resources Director
Ipsos
Paris, France

"Mark and I got to know one another as business colleagues during the merger of two very different companies, Markem and Imaje. In virtually every encounter where we collaborated on a subject together, he offered a valued and unique contribution and consistently found workable solutions to what were often challenging situations. He has good vision regarding organizational strategies and a clear understanding of how to build comprehensive and aligned programs to support the company's business strategy. He is clearly an authority on human capital management and the role that people can play in making organizations successful."

Serge Kral
President
Markem-Imaje
Geneva, Switzerland

"Mark and I became acquainted when we worked as colleagues on The Conference Board's mid-market HR executive council. Mark has a strong understanding of business with a keen understanding of human capital and its role and value to an organization. His book strikes the right balance between insight and practicality. It's a great read for any business leader looking to align their business with a strong performance or a serious HR professional looking to have a smarter and greater impact on the organizations they're a part of."

Stacy Reyan
Executive Director, Human Resources
APCO Worldwide
Washington, DC

"I met Mark for the first time in 2006 when I was the VP of Sales at Markem-Imaje. It became immediately obvious to me that he's a seasoned business leader with thorough knowledge in a broad range of business topics. At that time, Dover had acquired Markem and the decision had been made to integrate both Markem and Imaje into one single new company, with the objective to become the differentiated market leader in our business space.

As with most mergers, people and management quality were among the most critical factors of success. Mark introduced the senior management team very quickly to Human Capital Management and guided us through the entire process of implementation. He knew well which subjects needed to be addressed without delay and which ones needed to progress at a slower rate to ensure maximum success, keeping in mind the key business priorities and constraints.

The implementation of Human Capital Management made a huge difference in the success of the integration process and in our ability to create the new Markem-Imaje. Mark was highly instrumental to this success as he coached and navigated the executive leadership team skillfully through the implementation of HCM.

In this book, Mark skillfully lays out the path for Human Capital Management just as he led us through the process at Markem-Imaje. I recommend this book to any CEO or senior leader as a fantastic educational tool to help better understand the benefits of Human Capital Management, and how it can lead to maximum success of an organization."

Christian Lefort
Deputy CEO
Dirickx Groupe
Congrier, France

Acknowledgements

Besides my parents, there are three people who have opened up major paths of opportunity in my life.

The first is my cousin Bill Salsbury, who is no longer with us. Bill's contributions to society, and in particular, to our hometown of Utica, New York were countless. In 2007, he was inducted into the Greater Utica Sports Hall of Fame for his impact and support to Utica's youth community. Check out the Hall of Fame website at **www.greater021ticasports.com** to learn more about his accomplishments. When I was a young boy growing up, Bill was responsible for making many opportunities available that gave me a chance to succeed in school, sports, and life.

Richie Joseph was my college baseball coach, and gave me the opportunity to receive a good college education. Now retired, he was a tremendous role model, with a disciplined approach to his work and athletics, and also a friend who cared about the well-being of his players. I was just one of many student-athletes that benefited from his guidance and friendship.

Ken Rohner, also now retired, became my mentor and friend as I advanced my career with Schlumberger Limited. He had the ability to make all those reporting to him feel special, like they were his favorite, without ever telling them so. He was a wise businessman, a true HR professional, and I learned much from him. Ken took me under his wing when I was a young manager, and his willingness to put me in "stretch" positions that I could grow into was largely instrumental in my development into a senior business leader.

I will always be grateful to these three men for their positive influence and contributions to my life.

Many thanks to the individuals who were kind enough to provide advice, constructive comments, and/or encouragement regarding the content and/or publishing of this book; namely,

Emily Abrams; Bob King and Susan Griebel of Goal/QPC, Dr. Mark Davis, Joe Colletti and Omar Kerbage; also much appreciation to Benjamin Allison of the law firm of Sutin, Thayer & Browne for his legal review.

Thanks to all the business leaders and colleagues who I've worked with over the years, and who've helped shape my perspective. While I've lost touch with many former coworkers and contemporaries as time has gone by, I have fond memories of the relationships we formed.

I'd also like to thank those who were kind enough to write their endorsements regarding my book and/or my experience as a business leader. They include Campbell Fitch, Armagan Akar, Keith Chrzanowski, Stacy Reyan, Serge Kral, and Christian Lefort. I respect and am honored to be associated with each one of them.

Many thanks to Gary Kunath, business entrepreneur, public speaker, and author, for his wise counsel and countless business discussions that have complemented our personal friendship all these years.

A special thanks to my niece, Sondra Zabroske for designing the book cover. Her flair for art and design accentuates her skills as a professional architect.

To my brother, Jim Salsbury, business consultant and well regarded faculty member at Bentley College, a special thanks for all the advice, contacts, stories, editing, and conversations (intellectual and otherwise), that have led up to the publishing of this book, as well as providing the kind words in the Forward. I'm blessed to have a brother that I've always regarded as one of my heroes.

I can't thank my editor and publishing advisor enough for her attention to detail, always encouraging and simultaneously pushing me to constantly improve my work. She's a gifted writer, editor, and literary talent, whose energy and enthusiasm is infectious and brings joy to those around her. She also happens to be my loving daughter, Samantha M. Salsbury, and I wouldn't have been able to complete this project without her.

Success comes from recognizing and acting
on opportunities that pass by,
whether obvious or obscure.
So keep your eyes wide open.

Section 1
The Emergence of "Human Capital Management" as a Discipline

Introduction:
The Human Capital Survey at
Markem Corporation

My mid-life crisis was in 2000, the millennium. At the time, I was in charge of HR for Schlumberger Limited's high technology group, Test & Transactions, approaching $2B in revenue, with 22 factories, 10 product centers, and 9,000 employees worldwide.

After travelling for business about 80% of the time for three consecutive years, I needed a change, and my life back. I loved my job and working at Schlumberger, but I missed being around my family every day. However, in the culture of Schlumberger, there was no viable solution that would allow me to continue in the company and be with my family more often. Late that fall, I accepted an offer to join Markem Corporation as VP of HR in January 2001. Markem Corporation was a privately held company in Keene, New Hampshire, two hours from Boston, with $400M in sales consisting of two separate operating companies and employees in more than 20 countries. The company had a record of solid growth and profitability, a strong management team with excellent credentials, and an employee-friendly atmosphere.

After 15 years with Schlumberger, I relished the opportunity to bring my knowledge and experience to Markem. In fact, during the first several months of 2001, the experiences there were like a breath of fresh air because the company wasn't burdened by the disadvantages of being publicly owned or having too much administration.

And then, like the rest of the USA, we were faced with the unfortunate events of 9/11 and its aftermath. As you probably recall, the recession came early and abruptly in 2002. All of a sudden Markem's operating costs were out of balance with its sales. Faced with an ominous outlook for the remainder of the year, we reluctantly proceeded with a layoff of about 30 people (~3% of the company's workforce) in the second quarter of 2002. By most mid-size or large company standards, a reduction of 30 people isn't a big number, but in its 90-year history Markem only had two prior reductions. In each of these cases, the company offered something called a VSP, a "voluntary separation program" where people volunteered to leave and received one month per year of service without a cap. Not bad right? In reality, because of the attraction of the VSP, very few people were actually laid off. They volunteered to leave once the VSP was offered.

But in 2002, there was to be no VSP program. Times were changing, and frankly, we didn't want to spend the money to incentivize people to leave. As you would expect, this decision went down like a lead balloon. To make things worse, a day after the layoff we learned that there were union organizers outside the entrance to the company parking lots, handing out leaflets. The day after, an anonymous letter was sent to the home addresses of about 100 employees suggesting a few of the company's vice presidents should have been let go. They named the newly hired VP of Sales and me as good candidates. Being the new kids on the block and still in the assimilation process with the company made us easy targets. Suddenly, I wasn't feeling so great about the new job.

A week later, we had another setback when one of the major national newspapers wrote a derogatory article about Markem Corporation and a number of other companies for transitioning our "defined benefit" pension plan to a "cash balance plan." The article was critical of cash balance plans, and accused companies using such plans of improperly reducing retirement benefits to employees and retirees. Markem had in fact changed its retirement plan about a year earlier, but it had done so lawfully and in a professional manner. Despite this fact, our employees were naturally upset and confused by this accusation of the company changing its pension plan illegally, and the damage had been done. We were faced with the perfect storm, and many people in our workforce quickly went from being loyal and appreciative to dissatisfied and angry.

Over the course of the days following the article, management took a number of steps to stop the bleeding of morale and motivation among our employees. We held employee communications meetings explaining the pension plan changes going over both points of view. We conducted management training for union organizing, and reminded our employees we were open to any ideas they might have to make Markem a better place to work.

Within a few weeks, the hostile climate began to abate, and our actions seemed to have put out the fire. But for me, the situation continued to be disturbing. Not having previously worked for a paternalistic, privately held company, it was difficult for me to conceptualize how a loyal workforce could become disenchanted so easily and so fast.

While I thought about this one day shortly after this series of events, another senior member of the management team came into my office with a suggestion, "Maybe we should do a job satisfaction survey," he offered. I was hoping the expression on my face didn't show my disagreement with his idea. Pausing to reflect, I asked him to let me think about it a bit, and we agreed to talk about the subject later that week. Even though I didn't think the timing was right to do a survey, to be fair, I wanted to consider it as objectively as possible, instead of reacting too quickly, and rejecting it.

Later that evening, when most of the employees had left for the day, I did some research, and surprisingly came across an employee survey company that provided something called a "human capital survey." A human capital survey doesn't ask employees whether they think their pay is right or whether they're happy in their jobs. Instead, this kind of survey asks questions that help determine whether employees are engaged in their work, whether the communication between employees and their supervisors is effective, and whether employees truly understand the organizational goals of the company. I thought more about it, and decided that the human capital survey wasn't such a bad idea after all. Starting that day, I began to think about, learn, and appreciate the concept of "human capital management" as a practice.

Chapter 1
What is "Human Capital Management?"

The term human capital management starts with "human capital" which is consistently defined and *"commonly referred to as the knowledge, skills and abilities (KSA's) staff possesses that enables them to function effectively within the scope of their jobs."*[1]

However, there's a wide range of definitions for "human capital management," most of them broadly stated and having to do with the mobilization of people in an organization. Interestingly, there's no globally accepted definition of the term, though there are a number of articles and books that cover the subject in one way or another.

The field of Human Capital Management is still in its developmental phase. It's no wonder then, that there isn't any universal definition or description of it. In my research, I've also found it surprising that very few people and organizations have exploited the concept of Human Capital Management as the next logical step in the evolution of Human Resources.

While the HR profession has been slow to discover Human Capital Management, there are some companies providing integrated software applications to help companies manage their HR systems, and they have latched onto the acronym "HCM." One example is Oracle, who calls its integrated suite of HR related data and information management system "Oracle Fusion Human Capital Management." Others have done the same, and in the world of Enterprise Management, "HCM" is becoming a standard acronym.

These software tools are useful and supportive in helping executives do trending, monitoring, tracking and managing data and information to make better decisions for their organization. But in my opinion, this isn't Human Capital Management, it's Human Capital Data Management. These software packages are only tools, albeit useful tools to manage data and information, not people.

Derek Stockley, a well-respected Australian consultant specializing in training, human resources, and performance management consulting says this about human capital management:

"The term human capital is recognition that people in organisations and businesses are an important and essential asset who contribute to development and growth, in a similar way as physical assets such as machines and money. The collective attitudes, skills and abilities of people contribute to organisational performance and productivity. Any expenditure in training, development, health and support is an investment, not just an expense." [2]

With that said, Human Capital Management is different than Human Resource Management, and for the purpose of establishing a clear view of the difference between the two, it's necessary to compare them. In its Glossary of HR Terms, the Society for Human Resource Management (SHRM) defines Human Resource Management as follows:

"The formal structure within an organization responsible for all the decisions, strategies, factors, principles, operations, practices, functions, activities and methods related to the management of people." [3]

Another definition is provided by Edward L. Gubman, who wrote in the Journal of Business Strategy, *"the basic mission of human resources will always be to acquire, develop, and retain talent; align the workforce with the business; and be an excellent contributor to the business. Those three challenges will never change."* [4]

While Gubman's description is straightforward and aptly describes the overall mission of HR, in my opinion it's not ambitious enough in capturing the notion that **human capital, through its collective skills, knowledge and abilities, is the most important asset an organization has.**

The Charter Institute for Personnel and Development in London is the best write-up I've seen distinguishing the two:

"Human capital management is comprehensive because it includes not only human resource (HR) practices, but also other work practices and people management strategies that increase organizational performance. The important distinction between human resource management and human capital management is that human capital extends well beyond the HR function to encompass the total people strategy of the organization. Human capital is owned by all of the business leaders and resides with everyone in the

organization." [5]

What I like most about this perspective is that it distinguishes Human Capital Management as an organizational entity, not a functional entity. Additionally, it encompasses the various people practices that make up the whole of the organization, and in doing so, makes the case that Human Capital Management should be viewed as a distinct and separate discipline.

Therefore, Human Capital Management should be viewed as a tangible practice within an organization, and this is the reason why the phrase is capitalized throughout this book.

For the purpose of providing a foundation for Human Capital Management as an emerging practice, I have offered my own definition and description:

"Human Capital Management is an organizational practice by which the human capital assets of an organization are collectively leveraged to gain a competitive advantage. This view of Human Capital Management highlights the importance of taking a systematic approach to integrate and align important organizational elements to effectively drive human capital initiatives. This approach is what I call the Human Capital Management System."

Human Capital Management has a number of unique attributes:

1) **Human Capital Management is centered on programs and services based on key organizational initiatives, rather than individual or small sets of activities designed to improve efficiency and effectiveness of daily operations. In other words, Human Capital Management is broader than Human Resources, larger in scope, and beyond the sole domain of HR or any other function of the organization.** For example, staffing for engineering positions is a Human Resource activity while a workforce planning capability that results in a forecasting model and multi-year hiring plan is a Human Capital Management activity.

2) Human Capital Management is concentrated on the interrelationships of key organizational elements, and how

7

they work together. For example, in developing a Six Sigma program, a company's Human Capital Management perspective would include efforts to put in place supporting links to the Six Sigma program that would be well beyond the actual implementation of Six Sigma processes and tools themselves. There would be a need for cultural adaptations to be built into the organization, and perhaps compensation programs would need to be modified. Job structures and competencies might need to be updated as well. For Six Sigma to be properly applied, multiple organizational components need to be integrated so they can support one another within a system. **Human Capital Management takes a systems-based approach that links important elements of the organization, regardless of functional ownership**.

3) Continuous measurement of return on investment (ROI) and other key metrics should be a part of Human Capital Management. **Certainly it's useful to measure activities and outcomes to evaluate progress against results, but Human Capital Management relates to higher-level business goals, not tactical metrics.** For example, a good Human Capital Management metric for ROI might be a comparison of Revenue/Labor costs or Operating Earnings/Labor costs. At the functional level, the same type of higher-level ROI can be applied, for instance, by measuring the output of an engineering organization using an example such as the number of new products brought to market within three years. Of course, the challenge with high level ROI measurements is that it's often difficult to directly correlate actions to results since there can be multiple factors that influence results. What's important to take away from this is that measurements need to be put in place before the human capital initiative is started, and then progress needs to be gauged going forward for continuous improvement.

4) **In Human Capital Management companies, consistent day-to-day performance is a basic requirement for a business to be successful, but operational excellence is not the added value of Human Capital Management. The real contribution comes from the organization's ability to deliver company-wide and strategic performance. This will push the company to its desired state more quickly and to a greater extent.** This added value contribution of Human Capital Management can come in the form of culture or change management, performance management systems or other large-scale cross-functional efforts that will impact the company's performance significantly. A good example might be how to improve a performance culture within a company that needs to compete more effectively in its competitive space.

5) Last, but not least, **Human Capital Management is more about increasing revenue than it is about reducing costs**. In Human Capital Management, the emphasis is on projects related to revenue growth, as they're often more meaningful to a company's long-term success than cost cutting. An example of this principle took place in a company that I've become familiar with in the past several years. During 2009, the company's management conceived of a new customer sales and service model designed to improve sales channel management globally. The cross-functional team working on the project rewrote organizational roles and responsibilities, and outlined key selling processes. The roles and overall customer relationships between the company's customers and the internal Marketing and Customer Service organizations were impacted as well. In total, the initiative resulted in a refocused customer approach organizationally restructured to better align with the company's industry and customer target base. This Human Capital Management endeavor enabled the company to engage more effectively with its customers and understand their needs better, thereby leading to improved retention of sales, and a much better plan for addressing new customer sales activities.

Chapter 2
Human Capital as a
Competitive Advantage

Over the last decade, the growing importance of human capital has become obvious. It seems that each year The Conference Board's *"CEO Challenge: Top 10 Challenges"* survey includes human capital subjects such as "talent gaps" or "succession planning" in the list. The reasons for human capital's rise in importance are varied, and while it's not my intent to capture them all, it's worth noting a few:

- As government rules and regulations have become more complex, the need for specialization has increased. We depend greatly on individuals that we hire to perform specialized jobs, and we spend valuable resources to train and develop them. Therefore, the importance of hiring and retaining people with these specialized skills is much greater today than it was in the past.

- As the global economy makes it easier to do business internationally and at the click of a computer, competition can come from anywhere at anytime, and it's more difficult to protect niche markets. This in turn, places greater emphasis on the human capital of an organization to find new and innovative ways to retain customers and gain new ones.

- As technology has advanced, IT structures and systems that enable tools and processes to drive business have actually made it easier for companies to keep pace with their competitors. In the past, companies could maintain an advantage for a longer period of time based on their ability to develop proprietary tools and processes in sales and marketing, supply chain management or research and development. In many cases, these tools were well kept secrets and internally maintained, making it difficult for competitors to replicate. Today, it's a different story. If you want to become a "lean" company for example, there are a number of consultants who can help you install a continuous improvement system. Virtually every Enterprise Resource Planning (ERP) system offers embedded tools and processes to link business functionalities or you can find a compatible application service provider (ASP) for those functional requirements that are necessary to integrate.

What is the significance of these points?

Simply stated, while extraordinary products and unique services still afford a competitive advantage (for a limited period of time), the one advantage that stands the test of time... is people.

Consider these points:

- As the baby boomer generation exits the working world (even if it has been slowed due to a lengthy economic recession in the past decade), demographics experts predict there will not be enough qualified managers to fill the positions that will be available. Therefore, available talent will be a critical factor in an organization's success.

- Few companies are clever and talented enough to maintain a competitive advantage by having breakthrough products and services. As such, it has become increasingly more difficult to differentiate oneself from the competition over a prolonged period of time, and specialized and/or quality talent will be harder to come by.

- As foreign companies operate successfully in our domestic markets, and local companies go overseas to expand, it's becoming more difficult to sustain long-term double-digit growth in geographic markets.

- As companies reduce time to market or decrease product costs by using tools and processes that are becoming more commonly used by multiple competitors, these too will become limited as competitive advantages.

Organizations that thrive and survive will have a common advantage others will not have: the right people. Even understanding that there will always be those companies who have the best level of innovation and ability to make a better product, it's because they have the right people that they can do this in the first place.

Given the surplus of literature on a wide-range of topics associated with people as a competitive advantage, it should be no surprise that human capital is the center-point of most, if not all, organizational business strategies. Yet, despite this awareness, few organizations have taken strategic, comprehensive, and significant actions to make human capital their most important priority.

Why are so few companies proactively seeking to leverage their human capital?

In my view, there are three primary reasons:

While difficult to believe, many companies haven't recognized that human capital isn't a commodity. These companies haven't made human capital an important part of their business plans, nor do they utilize human capital as a competitive weapon or tool.

Second, there is sometimes a disconnect between the understanding that many CEOs and senior managers have in what they want to accomplish with human capital, and what is required in the form of a systematic and synergistic commitment, and investment to achieve their strategies and goals.

And third, many companies are still unprepared from a management resource standpoint to tackle the human capital challenges they have. They don't have internal talent that is either capable or trained to drive Human Capital Management programs.

Unfortunately, most organizations still haven't embraced Human Capital Management as a critical organizational practice. Day-to-day priorities take place over strategic planning. Cost cutting takes place over investment planning. Justification of ROI for investment in Human Capital Management programs takes precedence over the obvious conclusion that without such investments, a company's business future may be in dire jeopardy.

So what can we do?

We need to start by understanding and accepting what functioning Human Capital Management can provide. Once senior managers embrace the concept that people are the one sustainable long-term advantage, more organizations will take the necessary steps to embrace Human Capital Management.

Someone needs to become the champion in recognizing that the transition to Human Capital Management is both needed and feasible. The most likely individuals for this role are either the CEO of the organization, the chief HR Officer, or another senior executive who sees the big picture. Mid-level managers can also be spark plugs for a drive towards Human Capital Management, but this requires an additional selling step in the management loop, whereby the mid-level manager must find an ally at the executive level to help carry the torch.

Next, companies must be willing to invest in Human Capital Management. Even when hard ROI metrics are a challenge to predict, organizations can examine before/after scenarios and track results and trends to determine whether Human Capital Management programs have achieved their goals. The reality is that Human Capital Management is not yet a well-recognized discipline, and there is very little data available to compare companies who take a formalized approach to Human Capital Management from those who do not. Nonetheless, few would argue that companies who can effectively motivate their workforce are more competitive than those companies who do not. Even considering the studies that have shown how "best companies to work for" have generally outperformed their peers, being a "best company to work for" doesn't necessarily mean it practices Human Capital Management.

Only when organizations take a formalized approach to Human Capital Management will they truly begin their journey to making their human capital a competitive advantage. Most of the human capital actions taken by organizations are deployed independently, and as such, they may not be as successful as intended. The Human Capital Management System advocated in this book outlines tangible elements that are linked and aligned, and can be utilized by any organization to ensure its human capital initiatives are successfully implemented.

The desire to transition to Human Capital Management should be a no-brainer for most companies, since it should be obvious that the workforce can become a sustainable advantage for organizations. But transforming an organization to Human Capital Management is not simply a matter of attempting to hire the best people and expecting them to magically outpace the competition. Any sports advocate knows that you can have the best team, but there are several factors including team chemistry, a good game plan, motivational leadership, and so on, that turn a group of strong players into a championship team. There are many sports championships that have been won by teams that weren't the most talented.

To become a Human Capital Management organization, a blueprint or roadmap is needed. This book is your roadmap to Human Capital Management. In it, you will find the necessary steps and guidelines to help you navigate your organization through the transition.

Chapter 3
Prerequisites to Human Capital Management

Before moving to the transformation stage of Human Capital Management, let's examine some preliminary requirements that need to be established.

First and foremost, the most critical prerequisite to Human Capital Management is a strong belief and support from the CEO. Without this, the ability to move human capital to or near the top of the strategic agenda is difficult, if not impossible. The way people are utilized and valued in a company starts with the CEO. No matter what the values statement is, no matter what the stated culture, regardless of the marketing of people programs in the company, the CEO's commitment to his/her people is the key differentiator and speaks the loudest. The way he/she behaves with direct subordinates and others sets the tone both internally and externally about what is valued within the company, and what is not.

When Dover Corporation acquired my employer Markem, a senior executive from Dover named Bob Livingston came to visit us. Bob had just been assigned the responsibility of managing a group of companies, including ours, as a result of the reorganization of Dover. Prior to visiting our company headquarters for the first time, Bob had sent word that he wanted to spend time with the senior management team, first as a group, then with each executive individually.

Upon meeting with Bob one-on-one, I asked him about his views regarding the human capital of the organization, and it quickly became obvious to me that he understood the value of people, and the role they can play to help a company achieve its strategies and goals.

In our discussion, Bob talked about the people programs he had put into action, including one called DELLA (now Dover Corporation's executive leadership program) he had personally championed with Tina Sabin Governo, Dover's Vice President of Organizational Development.

After listening intently to Bob talk about his convictions regarding organizational and leadership development, the importance of management, and HR's role in the business, it was clear to me that he understood the true meaning of Human Capital Management.

Six months or so later, Bob Livingston was named President & CEO of Dover Corporation. One of his first key decisions upon becoming CEO was hiring Jay Kloosterboer as the first corporate VP of HR in Dover's history. Together, Bob and Jay began to put in place a number of human capital programs that have since made a positive and meaningful impact on the corporation's business and financial performance. Among these programs was the establishment of formal Dover values, leadership competencies, and a succession planning system. Rather than implement each one of these as separate programs, Dover regarded them as cogs within a comprehensive system, with the intent and commitment to make people one of Dover's competitive advantages. This example will be discussed in more detail in the chapter on Organizational Development.

Just as the CEO's commitment to Human Capital Management is critical, it's logical that his/her **direct subordinates, and in particular, the Chief Human Capital Officer, most often referred to as the VP of HR, must have the desire and capabilities to lead such a transformation.** This is the case because it's usually the Chief Human Capital Officer who needs to manage the human capital activities.

If the Chief Human Capital Officer or other senior executives already in place don't have the leadership capabilities to lead the transformation to Human Capital Management, the transition can happen, but the CEO will have to spend more time being involved in areas of the business that his/her subordinates should be managing. The alternative is replacement of key executives, but this will require additional time and organizational energy.

In any case, the CEO's commitment must be beyond a stated

personal belief or rhetoric. The CEO needs to take the time to articulate the rationale for the transition to Human Capital Management, and all that it entails. We'll review this point in more detail later in the chapter on Leadership.

The Chief Human Capital Officer must have a capable team with the potential to lead HR into a Human Capital transformation. Without strong HR people already in place, the time and effort to achieve this transition to Human Capital will be extended because it will be necessary for the Chief Human Capital Officer to rebuild his/her team, rather than mobilize them to work on Human Capital Management initiatives. Despite internally or externally posed obstacles, the new Human Capital team must be ready to demonstrate through commitment and perseverance that they're ready to lead the transition to a higher level of human capital organizational value.

Another important prerequisite for the transition to Human Capital Management is the "readiness" of the organization for this change. Using the analogy of Maslow's Hierarchy of Needs, the organization needs to ensure that physiological needs (metaphorically "food and shelter") are in place before attempting to reach self-actualization. In other words, an organization needs to perform its role in providing physiological needs to the organization, by ensuring the basic operational processes and functions are operating efficiently and effectively, before moving on to other higher-level value added activities. Examples of basic operations that need to be operating smoothly are sound management and performance of finance and accounting systems, management of quality, payroll administration, and so on.

Too many times I've seen various functions of an organization attempt to take on ambitious projects when the basic requirements of the function are not being met. One such example took place when I attended a combined meeting between Sales and Marketing for a company I consulted with. During the Marketing presentation, the VP of Marketing and a few other senior members of his team made presentations about what they wanted to achieve. The list was long and unrealistic. After completing his presentation, one of the Marketing managers asked the Regional Sales VPs if they were committed to partnering with Marketing to address a strategic goal that had been identified. After a long silent pause, one of the Regional Sales VPs responded that since Marketing wasn't delivering value as a tactical organization, why should he want to partner with them on a strategic basis?

While this response was a bit harsh and perhaps not the appropriate forum for the Sales executive to give the Marketing organization its performance appraisal, it was a powerful message that hit the Marketing organization head on in regards to its agenda. The message was clear: it's essential to satisfy tactical and basic requirements successfully before moving on to higher level challenges. This guideline should apply to every department within the organization, regardless of whether customers are internal or external.

Additionally, the "timing, scope, and size" has to be right for the transition to Human Capital Management. For example, it would seem poor timing for an organization to announce its plans to leverage human capital capabilities before, during or immediately after a layoff. This would obviously result in a lack of trust and credibility within the workforce regarding management's commitment to its people.

A timing decision also has to do with the number of other critical projects that are underway in the organization. If there are too many projects going on at one time, the organization's ability to digest them is reduced. The net result is the inability to gain support and traction, which will more than likely lead to organizational rejection via inertia or a watered down, saturated effect. The transition to Human Capital Management and the launch of a large-scale human capital initiative must be completed carefully because the risk of damaging your business is high if done poorly.

Another company I'm familiar with went through a transformation from being heavily decentralized to a more centralized structure. In making the change, management didn't attempt to wash away all of the aspects of the organizational culture that came with the decentralized structure. While there were definitely aspects of the company's culture that needed to be modified, there were other aspects of the decentralized culture that needed to be kept and reinforced. Take for example, the company's long-held commitment to having each operational unit own the relationship with the customer, something that was openly communicated by executives as being one of the traits that made this particular company special. Unfortunately, in operational terms, decentralization usually results in less efficiency. In companies that are very decentralized, operating units may be disconnected from other sister companies. This means that economies of scale are missing, and financial performance languishes below its potential.

In this case, senior management knew that in order to compete more effectively and increase its value as perceived by Wall Street, the bottom line would need to be improved. But corporate leadership didn't "throw the baby out with the bath water." They understood this decentralized approach was beneficial in each operating unit's competitive market space because it allowed its subsidiary companies to maintain their entrepreneurial spirit and commercial ownership. Instead of simply attempting to replace a decentralized operating culture with a centralized approach, leadership took more ownership of staff and support operations at the corporate level where real efficiencies could be gained through tangible corporate-wide projects. In doing this, they only centralized where large-scale projects could be employed to bring an advantage. This allowed the operating units to focus more time working on business development, marketing, sales, and all activities geared towards bringing them closer to their customers.

Second, understanding that there were many different strategic objectives to choose from, the management team was careful not to initiate too many projects in a short period of time that would overwhelm the organization and infrastructure. While still taking an aggressive position in launching the chosen initiatives deemed to be most important, the senior management team balanced the number and size of projects with their subsidiaries' ability to digest them culturally. Part of this consideration included an assessment of the organization's ability to manage them based on resource availability and skills, as well as the load being placed on the organization. The results have been successful to date, and the company is much more efficient than it was five years ago. The share price has grown as well. Today, many analysts regard it as a well-managed company with a good upside.

The story of Home Depot during the period of 2001-2007 is another example worth looking at in the context of "timing, scope, and size" of human capital initiatives and other strategic goals. This story has been well-documented, and in particular via an article written by Robert J. Grossman, titled, *"Remodeling HR at Home Depot"* and published in HR Magazine (November 2008). In his article, Grossman outlined the well-publicized saga of Home Depot's rollercoaster ride with Bob Nardelli, who was brought into Home Depot as CEO in 2001 from GE. You may recall some of the large-scale and ambitious goals Nardelli launched during that time, the most important one being his decision to dramatically shift the company's culture from that of decentralized store management to one where corporate management control became the dominating cultural force in the company. In a culture that had formerly given the power to the stores, within a short period of time, Nardelli dramatically altered the operations of the company with mandated controls, metrics, and management discipline at the corporate headquarters level.

Shortly after joining Home Depot, Nardelli brought in a new HR leader, Dennis Donovan, also a former GE executive. In addition to establishing new HR structures and operational approaches, Donovan was successful in gaining Nardelli's approval to dedicate an HR management representative in every one of Home Depot's 1,300 stores. This was a dramatic shift in culture as HR had previously been the responsibility of store management.

There were other major changes that took place, and in total, the culture shock that hit Home Depot was abrupt and substantial. Unfortunately, the number and scale of the changes that Nardelli brought to Home Depot kept the company in a state of conflict throughout his tenure, and the share price remained flat, despite increased sales and profits. In January of 2006, Nardelli left Home Depot. Within one month, Donovan left as well. In spite of improved sales and earnings, some people familiar with this story would support the view that Nardelli's time at Home Depot wasn't a success.

Why is this the case?

No doubt, many of Nardelli's changes were logical and some would argue necessary. Others would say that he tried to do too much within a short period of time. Some would say his management style didn't work within a company whose culture was so directly opposite than the one he was trying to build.

Perhaps most insightful is the commentary made in Grossman's story by one of Home Depot's regional executives at the time, who referred to Frank Blake's (Nardelli's replacement as CEO) approach as follows: *"Blake is reaffirming our focus on our core values. ... The culture has shifted back to realizing we are a retail company that needs to focus on customers."* 6

This is an astute observation, as any decision to dramatically change the strategy of the company requires a preliminary look back to the mission, vision, values, and culture. By doing this, it allows the decision makers to do a better job of assessing the risks vs. rewards in planning organizational strategies and objectives.

There's no question that Robert Nardelli and Dennis Donovan were seasoned executives who'd been successful at GE and understood the concepts of Human Capital Management. It's also likely though, that they may have underestimated the important links required to connect the actions derived from their business strategy back to the foundation of the company: its mission, vision, values, and culture.

Or perhaps what they missed was the understanding between the relationships and balance required in the number, size, and timing of the strategic and human capital initiatives that were launched.

There's no magic formula to determine how far one can push the system in remaking an organization or in launching a human capital initiative that will positively affect the company's performance. But an analysis should be made in regards to timing, scope, and the size of these initiatives before decisions are made to go forward.

If the assessment of an organization's readiness for Human Capital Management shows that the organization isn't ready to move forward, the root cause should be examined and addressed. If the assessment analysis shows that the organization is ready to move forward, then it's time to get on with the business of applying the elements of the Human Capital Management System. We will review this implementation in the following sections of this book, starting with The Business Foundation.

Section 2
Human Capital Management as a System

In Human Capital Management, mobilizing an organization to achieve large-scale goals requires a "systems" based approach. To be clear about the meaning, let's examine the definition of the word "system."

According to BusinessDictionary.com, a system is *"an organized, purposeful structure regarded as a whole and consisting of interrelated and interdependent elements (components, entities, factors, members, parts, etc.). These elements continually influence one another (directly or indirectly) to maintain their activity and the existence of the system, in order to achieve the goal of the system."* [7]

In Human Capital Management, the alignment of these elements is crucial for maximum benefit. This is an essential operating principle. The fully mobilized Human Capital Management System is much more powerful in driving workforce momentum than any single part of the System itself.

There are four components that make up the Human Capital Management System. When operationally in sync, they can have a substantial impact on an organization's results. The first of these is the "business foundation," consisting of an organization's mission, vision, values, and culture. In this section we will review each of the four elements of the business foundation independently, and how they're related to one another. We'll also cover the relationship between the business foundation and the "business strategy." This is depicted on the next page in Figure 1 and will be further discussed in Chapter 8.

Figure 1

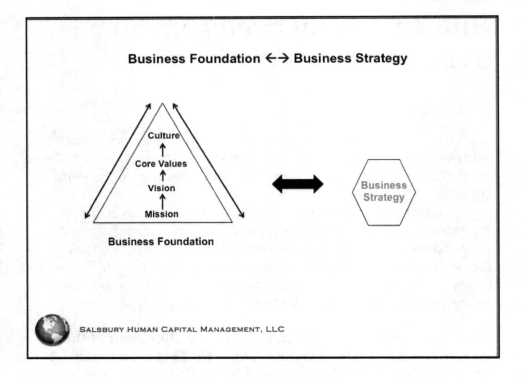

We'll look closely at the second key ingredient in the Human Capital Management System as well: the link between the "business strategy" and "organizational goals," and then "human capital initiatives." This is shown in Figure 2 below.

Figure 2

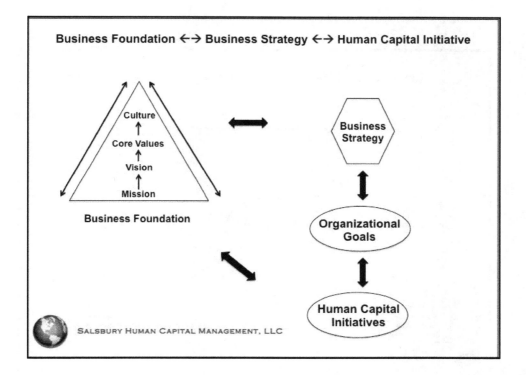

The third portion of the Human Capital Management System is what I have termed the Human Capital Management Wheel or "performance wheel" shown in Figure 3 below. I call this the performance wheel because the spokes of the wheel generate action-oriented programs and activities leading to intended results. This performance wheel will be reviewed in detail in Section 3.

Figure 3

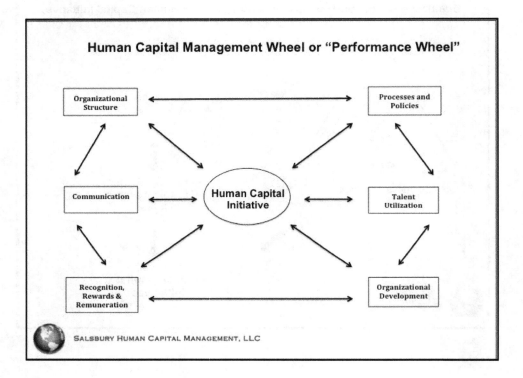

The fourth element influencing the success of the Human Capital Management System is leadership required from the CEO, addressed in Section 4 of this book. HR's role is also covered in this section. The complete Human Capital Management System is shown in Figure 4 below.

Figure 4

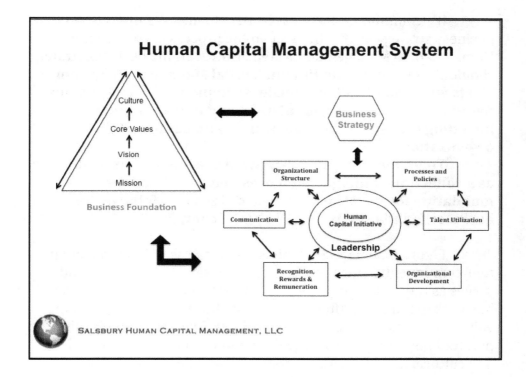

Chapter 4
The "Business Foundation"
Comes First

It's common for business leaders to mistakenly focus on business strategy as the first step in the process of constructing a Human Capital Management System. However, the business strategy shouldn't come first. **The Human Capital Management System starts with what I call the "business foundation." The business foundation consists of four distinct and unique ingredients including the mission, vision, values, and culture of the organization.**

Together, they articulate what the business is about, and as a collection of integrated pieces, they establish the foundation for the strategy and activities that follow. The business foundation is the DNA of the company.

Figure 5 on page 29 depicts the business foundation and its four components. The mission is at the base of the pyramid, and serves as the underpinning for the other three dimensions of the business foundation. After the mission, the vision is next, then the values, and finally, organizational culture. The arrows inside the pyramid point upwards from mission to vision, and then to values and culture, to indicate the order that each should be crafted.

Figure 5

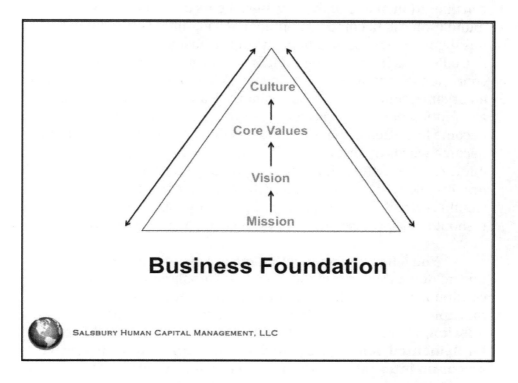

Articulating the ingredients of the business foundation in this particular order is key for the following reasons. **First, it's always better to have a baseline of where you are (mission) before considering where you'd like to go (vision). Hence, the mission comes before the vision, which logically comes before the business strategy. This allows for determination of the gap between the mission and vision, prior to definition of the business strategy and organizational goals.**

Likewise, the values of the company should match and support the mission and vision. Take for example, a technology business that relies on speed and time to market. Establishment of "innovation" as a value would certainly make sense for this company if new ideas in a fast-paced technological and competitive environment were central to its success. It would also seem logical for the same company to grow a culture where speed is a key factor for success.

It's easy to see how a company that sets its course without consideration of one of the key ingredients of the business foundation can become disjointed in its alignment. The same misalignment can occur when one of the business strategy ingredients is in the wrong sequence. This naturally leads to confusion in messages to employees. What most often occurs when an organization works on its business strategy without starting with a definition of its business foundation is the mission and vision become forgotten or not well understood by employees. Values just become words or slogans that few people actually believe or even know exist, and the culture of the company takes on a life of its own, or more likely, is fashioned after the ideologies of the CEO. The CEO should certainly have a say regarding an organization's culture, but it should be a professionally developed and vetted process.

You'll note in Figure 5 that the arrows outside the chart point up and down the sides of the pyramid. This signifies that there's a continuous and ongoing relationship and connection between these four components and the impact they have on one another. **Once the mission, vision, values, and culture have been created and implemented, it's a good practice to examine them sequentially and as an integrated system to check for alignment. This is beneficial because it provides a logical and credible story the workforce can understand and accept as the basis by which they will operate.**

Consideration of adjustments in any one of the business foundation parts should be carefully thought out in advance, and not be taken lightly. Nor should they be changed often or easily. It takes time and repetition for behaviors to be consistently applied and for cultures to be ingrained in an organization. Substantial or frequent changes in the business foundation will only confuse people as to what's expected and where the organization is headed. As such, careful thought needs to be put into determining whether and when to change the mission, vision, values, and culture, with the understanding that each needs to be realistic, current, and consistently applied.

Each of these four business foundation ingredients will now be reviewed individually as elements of the Human Capital Management System.

Chapter 5
Mobilization of the Workforce Starts with the Mission and Vision

As defined in Business.Com, a written mission statement is *"a written declaration of an organization's purpose and focus that normally remains unchanged over time. Properly crafted mission statements (1) serve as filters to separate what is important from what is not, (2) clearly state which markets will be served and how, and (3) communicate a sense of intended direction to the entire organization."* [8]

A written vision statement is *"an aspirational description of what an organization would like to achieve or accomplish in the mid-term or long-term future. It is intended to serve as a clear guide for choosing current and future courses of action."* [9]

Some people get the mission and vision statements mixed up. The simplest way to understand the difference between them is that the mission statement is what's to be accomplished today or in the present state, and a vision statement is what's to be accomplished in the future. More often than not, vision statements are internally used while mission statements are used both internally and externally.

Many companies have mission and vision statements, but sometimes they're developed haphazardly, hurriedly or by one or two of the senior managers of the company. Together, the mission and vision should be the rock on which the organization is built. Therefore, their creation and articulation should not be taken lightly. If a company doesn't deeply examine its purpose and what it's trying to become, then everything that follows could easily be out of alignment.

From my perspective, senior management should work as a team in carefully outlining mission and vision statements for two very good reasons:

1) **To provide direction to an organization in articulating and then forging the identity that's been defined for the organization, and**

2) **To provide a foundation or grounding for establishing a business strategy, that is, understanding where the company is today versus where management wants the company to be in the future.**

Let's look at an example of a company mission statement.

Patagonia is a privately held company headquartered in Ventura, California. Yvon Chouinard, an adventurous rock climber and surfer, started it more than 30 years ago. For the reader who doesn't know the story of Patagonia, I invite you to visit their website to learn more about this fascinating success story. When you go to the company's website, **www.Patagonia.com**, click on Company Information, and you'll find the following page:

"Our Reason for Being"
"Build the best product, cause no unnecessary harm, use business to inspire and implement solutions to the environmental crisis. – Patagonia's Mission Statement

Patagonia grew out of a small company that made tools for climbers. Alpinism remains at the heart of a worldwide business that still makes clothes for climbing – as well as for skiing, snowboarding, surfing, fly fishing, paddling and trail running. These are all silent sports. None requires a motor; none delivers the cheers of a crowd. In each sport, reward comes in the form of hard-won grace and moments of connection between us and nature. Our values reflect those of a business started by a band of climbers and surfers, and the minimalist style they promoted. The approach we take towards product design demonstrates a bias for simplicity and utility. For us at Patagonia, a love of wild and beautiful places demands participation in the fight to save them, and to help reverse the steep decline in the overall environmental health of our planet. We donate our time, services and at least 1% of our sales to hundreds of grassroots environmental groups all over the world who work to help reverse the tide. We know that our business activity – from lighting stores to dyeing shirts – creates pollution as a by-product. So we work steadily to reduce those harms. We use recycled polyester in many of our clothes and only organic, rather than pesticide-intensive, cotton. Staying true to our core values during thirty-plus years in business has helped us create a company we're proud to run and work for. And our focus on making the best products possible has brought us success in the marketplace."[10]

Written in story-teller fashion, Patagonia's mission statement provides the reader with a pretty clear view of what the company is all about: building great products, doing no unnecessary harm to the environment, and using business as a tool to improve the environment. The statement and supporting description are simple and clear enough for Patagonia's workforce to understand and describe plainly to anyone who were to ask them.

A company's mission statement needs to be written for the benefit of its employees. In my career, I've seen senior managers and/or marketing people craft the mission statement, only to communicate it to the workforce and then never use it again...until they realize that it's outdated. When this happens, the mission statement is either a waste of time or isn't being used effectively enough to help forge a common identity and mission for the workforce to follow. Worse yet, the result is that few people even know what their company's mission is. This is indeed unfortunate because the mission statement is the starting point and first step in erecting the business foundation.

Just as the mission statement is a building block in establishing the business foundation, the vision statement is another key component because it sets a broad direction for the organization's ambition for the future. Expressing the mission and vision presents an opportunity for the organization to evaluate the gap between where it is and where it wants to be.

As noted earlier, many companies don't share their vision statements externally. The most obvious reason for this is that they don't want current or potential competitors to know their future direction.

For those companies who do publicly share their vision statement, they normally don't provide enough detail in words or information to disclose competitive details. Let's take the example of Coca-Cola's vision statement:

"Our Vision"
"Our vision serves as the framework for our Roadmap and guides every aspect of our business by describing what we need to accomplish in order to continue achieving sustainable, quality growth.

- *People: Be a great place to work where people are inspired to be the best they can be.*
- *Portfolio: Bring to the world a portfolio of quality beverage brands that anticipate and satisfy people's desires and needs.*
- *Partners: Nurture a winning network of customers and suppliers, together we create mutual, enduring value.*
- *Planet: Be a responsible citizen that makes a difference by helping build and support sustainable communities.*
- *Profit: Maximize long-term return to shareowners while being mindful of our overall responsibilities.*
- *Productivity: Be a highly effective, lean and fast-moving organization."* [11]

In the case of Coca-Cola, the company openly states that their vision serves as the framework for their future roadmap and business planning. While none of the 6Ps listed in Coke's vision statement are specific enough to give away confidential information, they do provide the following benefits to the company and its employees:

- Each of the statements provides a baseline for the company and its subsidiaries to pursue actions that are consistent with the vision.

- While six statements are at the high end of a person's recall ability, they are easier to remember because of the "6P" gimmick that is used to describe them.

As the Coca-Cola Vision illustrates, the vision statement can be a valuable ingredient of the business foundation because it sets the direction for business planning.

The mission and vision statements are fundamental actions that should be examined prior to updating the business strategy. A company that moves forward in developing a business strategy without first evaluating the mission/vision risks disconnecting the two. A company that doesn't take the time to realistically understand where it is in the present state will more than likely have difficulty in understanding what the gap is between where it is today and where it needs to go in the future. As a consequence, misalignment is more likely to occur, and the organization may chase short-term interests regardless of its strategy.

Chapter 6
Values: Guiding Organizational Conduct

The third component of the business foundation is the "values" of an organization. The most straightforward definition I've seen for "values" is from the website of the U.S. National Park Service:

"The core values of an organization are those values we hold which form the foundation on which we perform work and conduct ourselves. We have an entire universe of values, but some of them are so primary, so important to us that throughout the changes in society, government, politics, and technology they are STILL the core values we will abide by. In an ever-changing world, core values are constant. Core values are not descriptions of the work we do or the strategies we employ to accomplish our mission. The values underlie our work, how we interact with each other, and which strategies we employ to fulfill our mission. The core values are the basic elements of how we go about our work. They are the practices we use (or should be using) every day in everything we do."[12]

I especially like this definition because it reminds us that values should be the foundation for the way the internal organization works.

Values represent the beliefs that an organization has, and should guide the internal conduct of the employees in the company. They reflect the company's personality both internally and externally, and influence behaviors and actions of employees with their co-workers, vendors, and customers. Values are also meaningful because they have a direct impact on an organization's culture.

As mentioned earlier, the mission and vision of an organization should be defined before the company's core values. When the values support and are consistent with the mission and vision, it's easier for the workforce to relate to them. **Some organizations make the mistake of establishing values as a separate exercise from the development of its mission and vision. In organizations that practice Human Capital Management, the values of the organization are effectively aligned with the mission and vision in a way that can be leveraged for organizational momentum and consistency.**

Too often, managers work according to their own beliefs and unilaterally change expected organizational behaviors based on the behavior of managers above and around them. When this occurs, the intended values are replaced with unintended behaviors. Recently, I spoke with an employee whose manager informed him that the harsh management style he used was a result of the "needs of the business," rather than a personal management style. One of the values of this particular company is "Respect for People." This means that either the manager disregarded the values of the company and replaced them with his own management style or somewhere along the line "Respect for People" was lost in translation. Either way, the end result was a dissatisfied and demotivated employee who became confused in understanding what the company said versus what the company (represented by the manager) did.

Another example of values in action is one that took place many years ago when I was a manager at a large corporation. The company had gathered 100 of its senior USA managers for a two-day meeting in Atlanta. At the start of the meeting, the company's chairman conducted a full two-hour session on the company's values, one of which was "people are our greatest asset." The presentation consisted of only one overhead slide that showed the values written in simple language, but the chairman's narrative included various real-life company stories and examples showing these values in action within the company. While he had no doubt rehearsed and given this presentation multiple times prior to this particular occasion, his enthusiasm and commitment to the company values and the meaning behind them were obvious to the participants in the room. It was very motivating for me as a manager in the company, and his approach inspired me to reinforce these values with others in my own team and organization.

An even more vivid recollection comes from what happened at the conclusion of that meeting when the chairman and a few of his senior level direct reports held a roundtable discussion where managers could ask questions and discuss key business issues. In this question and answer session, one of my colleagues had apparently asked a question one of the senior executives didn't care for. As a response to the question, and in front of this large group of managers, the executive ridiculed my unsuspecting peer for posing this question.

At that moment, the chairman, who had the size and presence to command anyone's attention, stood and held up his hand, making it clear that it was time for the other senior manager to stop talking. The room became quiet and subdued as he matter-of-factly reminded the offending senior executive of the values of the company right on the spot. He further commented that it was senior management's responsibility to treat all employees of the company with dignity and respect, regardless of their opinions.

In observing this exchange, the most impressive aspect was the chairman using his subordinate's miscue as a real-time teaching moment for everyone in attendance, especially the offending senior executive. While he was directly calling out the subordinate executive, the chairman did so with respect and in a lighthearted manner. It was a valuable lesson for everyone in the room, especially the other senior manager, who, quite frankly, needed many more lessons about how to treat people than the one given that day.

These two examples show how **human behavior can unintentionally hinder the reinforcement of values within an organization. Actions directly impact the way values are understood and reinforced in an organization, whether they come in the form of communications, policies or processes.**

I am reminded of an industrial B2B company I was familiar with who had "innovation" as a value. There were a number of built-in operational road-blockers in the company that got in the way of innovation to the point where rank-and-file employees felt that innovation wasn't deemed important at all. Approval levels in the company were constrained and written in exhausting detail. Many decisions were deferred to higher reporting levels, and as a result it was common for meaningful actions within the organization to be slow and time consuming. The company didn't view university recruiting as a key innovation tool, and as such, most of the engineers in the company were mid-career hires. The CEO of the company was known for his tendency to reject innovation projects that didn't have immediate payback. As you can tell, the company was risk averse in several ways.

Unfortunately, there was a strong disconnect between the "innovation" value and the actions of the company to support it. Innovation may have been one of the values in times past, but it had lost its role as a value under this management team. In this case, the actions and personality of the company had drifted away from its original intent. The result was confusion and disillusionment among employees throughout the organization who were being told one thing, but saw another through conflicting management actions.

It's a good practice to regularly examine the alignment between the mission, vision, and values, and then reinforce them through tangible, desired behaviors that are associated with those values. This will ensure that the values have the intended meaning within the organization.

Chapter 7
The Glue that Binds the Organization Together

The fourth critical ingredient in the Business Foundation is the "organizational or company culture," and is defined as *"... the sum total of an organization's past and current assumptions, experiences, philosophy, and values that hold it together, and is expressed in its self-image, inner workings, interactions with the outside world, and future expectations. It is based on shared attitudes, beliefs, customs, express or implied contracts and written and unwritten rules that the organization develops over time and that worked well enough to be considered valid."* [13]

Many people simply refer to organizational culture as the glue that holds an organization together. It's commonly understood as the beliefs and values that drive organizational behavior, and define how business is conducted each day.

Too often, culture is thought of as a "soft" part of the business, and therefore, is not tangibly identified in writing and communicated formally within the organization. Nevertheless, culture can be identified easily if one looks closely at the organization's key characteristics or attributes.

There are plenty of models regarding the traits that make up an organizational culture. While I don't intend to debate the merits of these models, I've assembled a short list of what I believe to be the criteria that shape an organization's culture:

Key attributes of company culture:

1) The degree of **formal hierarchy** within the organization: Is it acceptable for an employee to send an email or visit the CEO of a company or is it more likely that this type of communication is taboo? What other formal or informal rules demonstrate a company's approach to how individuals at different levels of the company interact with one another?

2) The **relative importance of cost, time, and quality** in the organization: What is the urgency and speed within the organization, especially with respect to the need for data/information prior to a decision being made? Do the organization's key decision makers pull the trigger on decisions with 75% of relevant data/information or do they need more information? Is there a frenzied pace in daily operations? Is the organization more people oriented (feeling) in its decision-making or task oriented (thinking)? Is urgency and speed something that comes up in performance reviews? What's the relative importance in the achievement of short-term versus long-term financial or other business results?

3) The **power structure** in the organization: Who makes the decisions? Where is "autonomy" and "delegation" on the decision-making continuum? Who or what functions have organizational influence in the company?

4) The way **people communicate** with one another: How assertive, aggressive or pushy are people in the way that they work with one another? Is the culture one of conflict avoidance where polite interactions are valued more or less than a company where conflict is welcomed and valued as a means to achieve the best results?

5) The **degree of formalization** in the way that business is conducted: Is the organization heavy on rules and written communications? How much is process management used in day-to-day operations?

6) The extent to which there are written or unwritten **customs and traditions** that are followed in the organization: Who gets to park where in the company parking lot? What are the normal hours people work in the company in order to be seen as hard-working employees? Is it common for people to work remotely? How are people rewarded, and what types of awards and ceremonies take place in the company? What do the written employment policies say about how the company works?

Very few companies actually take the time or make the effort to articulate their culture in writing. If they were to do so, many of these companies would find that the desired cultural attributes might not be well understood or even agreed upon by senior management. They might also find that the cultural attributes of the organization don't match with their stated values. Understanding this, it's a good practice to characterize the culture of the company by putting it in writing, and then communicate and reinforce it through actions.

Let me share an example from the merger that took place between Markem and Imaje in 2007-2008 that will reinforce the importance of ensuring values and culture are well connected.

Late in 2007, Markem had been acquired by Dover Corporation, and the decision had been made to merge Markem with Imaje Corporation, a French company Dover had acquired some years earlier. Both companies were in the product identification industry, selling printers and inks for marking and coding applications ranging from electronic chips to bags of potato chips.

During the preparation for the merger, the senior managers of the newly combined company, Markem-Imaje, wanted to carry forward into the new organization the best traits of the two companies. One of the strengths of Imaje was its "performance culture." Employees and managers were proud they'd achieved challenging financial objectives for a number of years.

Markem was also financially successful, but in my opinion, it didn't have as strong a performance culture as Imaje. It did however, have a strong "people" culture, and this was reflected in the collaborative and highly respectful ways employees worked together. Going forward with the merger, it was management's intention to create a culture that valued strong financial performance, but also a strong people culture. In doing so, the company came up with the following Markem-Imaje Values 14:

Our Values...

- **PEOPLE**: We share a common set of human values – to be accountable, to have integrity, to be honest, to always be professional; we treat people with care inside and outside the company in a way that differentiates us from our competitors.

- **EXCELLENCE**: "Performance Counts": We hold ourselves to the highest standards of performance and achievement of the Dover metrics; we are focused on the sustainability of our product identification solutions.

- **OUR CUSTOMERS:** We optimize teamwork, loyalty and a genuine concern for our customers; we are innovative, adaptable, reliable, passionate and dedicated to continuous improvement...and all of these behaviors together bring us customer intimacy.

To some managers in the company, these values of "people" and "excellence" were a contradiction. For those who achieved results through heavy-handed management, it was difficult for them to see how both values could coexist. For others who overlooked performance issues, they were confused and distressed by the need to be more forceful in pushing for higher job performance.

As you can imagine, it was not an easy cultural transition for some managers to make. For those who in the past had spent little time using positive motivational techniques in their management style, moving to a culture of being respectful and kind was risking the company's performance standard, and therefore, decreased odds of achieving excellence. For others who placed more emphasis on how people were treated, and were used to accepting satisfactory or even less than satisfactory performance, it was a challenge for them to make the transition to higher performance standards.

So, what did the new senior management team do to overcome this challenge?

The first action was to tell a compelling story that all employees could relate to. This started with creating mission and vision statements to reflect the company's purpose and view regarding the current mission, and what the vision was for the future. It was critical for the combined workforce to understand these two baseline ingredients of the business foundation. It was equally critical for them to understand the difference between where we were in our mission and where we wanted to be in our vision, relative to time and distance. In other words, how far were we from where we wanted to go, and how long would it take us to get there? In our messaging to employees, we informed them that to fully leverage and take advantage of the market opportunity the merger provided, we needed to work quickly and collectively to fill the gap between where we were and where we wanted to be. This explanation, along with the fact that we wanted to be number one in our competitive space, was the justification we used with our employees in explaining why it would be necessary to raise our performance standards within a short period of time. In delivering this message, we explained to the workforce the critical need for our "people" value to be a primary attribute in the eyes of our customers. We needed our workforce to embrace the principal that it was our people who made us special and unique as a business partner. This internal communication was developed and repeatedly communicated by senior management in presentations at various meetings held with different groups of employees throughout the company. Additionally, a video was made linking our mission, vision, values, and business strategy, and then it was communicated to all employees in the company.

Next we put together a training program around our company culture, which we nicknamed "4T" reflecting our external and internal marketing brand "The Team To Trust." This two-and-a-half day training program consisted of an opening session led by the CEO that spoke about our mission, vision, values, culture, and business strategy, using the same compelling rationale to gain commitment and create enthusiasm. The second section of the training program was about making our company culture real by pointing out ways in which the company culture would be manifested in the organization on a day-to-day basis. We gave examples of appropriate behaviors that employees could identify with as we outlined our culture. This was followed by a one-day session on change management, led by an outside vendor that was chosen mainly because of having worldwide experience on this topic. The last session of the training consisted of interactive exercises meant to encourage discussion of the values and culture. This further gave us feedback and built a dialogue with our employees on how to work together on the challenges that we faced going forward in the people side of the merger.

One of the significant points about this training program is that it didn't take months to prepare and organize. As an organization, we needed to gain momentum quickly and as such, speed was of the essence. With the assistance of the Marketing department and a small task force, a pilot program was launched in about two months time. To gain the maximum benefit, we chose a group of Sales and Service managers in the country where we saw the merger was going to be most challenging because of internal cultural differences between the two former companies.

This trial program enabled us to benefit in two ways. First, we knew that the selected group of participants would give us the kind of direct and open feedback we needed to improve our training program before implementing it globally. Second, we knew that the sooner we indoctrinated this particular group of managers with our new culture, the sooner we could affect change management behaviors in that region. This was important to do since it was this region where management and employee relations' problems were most prevalent.

Finally, we launched a new performance appraisal within several weeks of the merger's announcement in order to ensure our values and culture would match our desired behaviors. The new appraisal was designed by a team of managers from both companies, and led by key members of the Human Capital team (formally called "Human Resources" in both companies).

As one would expect, some members of the team working on the performance appraisal simply suggested editing the performance appraisals that were already in place within each company, attempting to blend them together. Others lobbied for the performance appraisal they liked best, which by coincidence was the one they were most accustomed to. After a little management encouragement though, the team's focus was quickly clarified as we asked them to provide us with a simple and basic tool reflecting the values and behaviors we were looking for from our employees around the world.

Fortunately, this team was a broad-based group of individuals and managers from different countries who could help us decipher language and cultural issues that needed to be corrected. Following its completion, the new appraisal met our objectives of being simple to understand, as well as being clear and crisp in linking performance ratings to criteria. The new performance appraisal was then communicated by the Human Capital team to management, and cascaded to employees throughout the company.

The new performance appraisal was the first win for the Human Capital team that had just been assembled following the merger. The timing of its launch was beneficial as well. As the merger took place in December 2007, the new performance appraisal was communicated in February 2008, shortly following the completion of appraisals that took place for the 2007 year. In training managers and employees on the new performance management tool, Human Capital explained that the new appraisals would be used to evaluate performance at the end of 2008. This meant that employees and managers would have almost a full year to work under the new values and culture of the company prior to having their performance appraised under the new approach.

This decision was well received and took the edge off of what could've otherwise been perceived as a potentially negative impact of the merger. Instead, employees viewed this approach as reasonable and rational, and it was difficult for the "negative few" to gain much momentum.

In a large-scale human capital initiative like a merger, it's critical that elements of the business foundation are well aligned before moving on to organizational strategy and goals. It's no secret that many mergers fail because management doesn't spend enough time on what some refer to as the soft side of the business. As the prior example shows, **the business foundation doesn't have to be soft and it shouldn't be. Alignment of the business foundation should be made through tangible and operational actions so that the workforce has a clear path to follow, whatever phase of the life cycle a company is in: start-up, growth, expansion or maturity.**

Now let's go back to the Markem Corporation story I wrote about in the Introduction of this book. With the completion of this story, I'd like to explain further what I mean by tangible and operational actions to support and reinforce the business foundation.

You will recall that it wasn't long after I joined Markem Corporation as VP of Human Resources in 2001 that the events of 9/11 preceded a full-fledged economic downturn in early 2002. It was during this time I recognized two very strong characteristics in the company culture. First, the employees of the company were very dedicated and proud to be Markem employees. As one of the largest employers in the state of New Hampshire, Markem had built a reputation as a top-notch employer, and one that people in the community were pleased to be associated with. Managers and employees at all levels were friendly and treated each other with dignity and respect. The overall work environment was one that was pleasant and fun. The company had kept its shareholders happy with profits that translated into reasonable dividends over the years.

At the same time, based on my experience, Markem was not a company with a high performance culture compared to publicly held companies who constantly seek to meet quarterly shareholder expectations. To me, this seemed to be a knowing compromise made by the owners who were happy to be able to provide employment and economic growth for the small city of Keene, and the state of New Hampshire, while still providing reasonable dividends to the shareholders.

Partially due to this benevolence, there was also an "entitlement" mentality within the company. Since management had taken good care of its employees for three generations with only two very minor employment reductions in the history of the company (founded some 90 years earlier in 1911), people generally expected that the company would take care of them going forward. While people were loyal and appreciative of what the company had done for them, many believed it was the company's responsibility to find ways to cut expenses and deal with the economic downturn of 2002 without cutting jobs. This was natural to expect, since it wasn't uncommon for those who didn't perform well in one position to be transferred to another job in the company where they might perform better.

There may still be some companies operating today who've been able to sustain this kind of lifetime employment approach, but Markem, even though it was privately held, was in a market that was becoming more consolidated. The top two players in the market were much larger companies, Videojet (owned by Danaher Corporation) and Imaje (owned by Dover Corporation). On top of the challenges brought on by Markem's position in the marketplace, the recession brought additional challenges that put pressure on the company to improve its ability to compete.

This combination of factors led senior management to take a number of actions to help the company become more competitive. As mentioned in the Introduction, one of these actions included a decision to implement a small reduction-in-force, trimming about 30 temporary and permanent full-time employees from the workforce as the company's operating costs weren't in line with its ability to generate revenue. As you can imagine, this type of decision would have negative implications in any company, let alone one that has a paternalistic history.

You will also recall the subsequent unfortunate actions that followed the reduction-in-force: the beginning of union organizing activities, an anonymous letter to employees suggesting that senior managers should've been among those laid off, and finally, the bad press the company received as a result of the newspaper article regarding its change in pension plan.

At the employee and management communications meetings that senior management held after the layoff, the questions and comments that came from both rank-and-file employees and middle managers were troublesome in their tone and content.

As a member of the senior management team, I wasn't surprised that the reduction-in-force resulted in disappointed and disheartened employees, but I was somewhat taken back by the level of distrust and bitterness that seemed to have appeared. After all, this was a company that had taken good care of its employees for decades.

As a relative newcomer to the senior management team, it disturbed me how such a loyal workforce could become disenchanted so quickly. As I reflected on the idea of conducting a human capital survey with our workforce, three thoughts came to my mind.

First, employees weren't clear about what our mission and vision was all about. I'm certain this was the case since we didn't have a mission or vision statement at the time.

Second, the majority of our workforce didn't understand the relationship between the importance of the company's achievement and their own well-being.

Third, our business environment and competitive position required that we make some fundamental changes in our "performance culture." Without taking steps to address these issues, I was concerned we wouldn't survive.

As some of the members of the senior management team discussed our predicament, we wholeheartedly agreed that for us to achieve our business goals, we were going to have to make some changes going forward. Knowing this, we took a number of steps over the course of the next year that focused on recalibrating and updating our company values.

There are plenty of companies who have values, and these are often displayed on the company's website or bulletin boards.

However, as you may know, many of these companies do little more than list these values, and don't take specific actions to reinforce them with their workforce. The reality is that you can walk into almost any workplace today, ask an employee what their company values are, and they won't be able to name them. I've done this in organizations I've worked in, and in other organizations I've visited. In most instances, the people in organizations where values weren't tangibly ingrained were not able to name what their company values were. In cases where people could list the values, most of the time they weren't able to explain their meaning.

Obviously, this is a telltale sign that the values aren't being used effectively to drive behavior in the company, and as such, the values are useless. They aren't contributing to the desired culture since they don't encourage desired employee behavior. Usually the result is that employees within the organization operate according to an underlying culture that is "values-less" or according to the whim or management personality of their supervisors and higher-ups. In these cases, it's more common for there to be conflicting behavioral traits. Consider the company that touts its "respect for people" value. When the value isn't communicated, reinforced or integrated operationally, it's forgotten. People don't take it seriously. Managers act according to their own beliefs and personalities, and employees do the same.

Markem had written values, but the company hadn't done much to communicate those values over the years. The decision to reintroduce company values was a decision that came out of necessity as a requirement for us to substantially improve our competitiveness, and to increase our morale. We did so by rewriting an updated version of the company values so they could be well understood, and then we supported them with stories and examples of these values in action. In all of our communications, we made it clear that for the company to thrive and survive, each of us needed to live up to the values and understand that without performance, we couldn't protect our future. We asked our employees to embrace changes that needed to be made, and made it clear that this was necessary for survival. In a way, this was the "burning platform" approach to change management. It was also necessary because there was no time to waste, and a dysfunctional and disillusioned workforce would only feed the disruption that had already occurred.

We then utilized a number of reinforcement approaches to

tangibly drive the values into the company. First, we built a management presentation around the values and presented them at every opportunity, including our monthly meetings with managers, and our quarterly meetings with all employees. Our values were also posted on bulletin boards, the company's website, and other logical places for our employees to see.

Next, I began to hold "roundtable lunches" every Friday with a dozen or so employees from different functions within the business. During these sessions I discussed the values, what they meant, and carried on a dialogue with the employees regarding our need to live the values in the way we worked. I also asked employees about their concerns and tried to address matters they brought up that needed fixing. These meetings were very beneficial as they gave us the opportunity to spread our management message. It was worthwhile to the employees who had a direct line to a senior manager in the company to pass on their grievances or concerns.

Additionally, we organized a one-day course for all employees called the "Fundamental Behaviors," a list of behaviors that were written to support and reinforce our values. In particular, we decided to zoom in on one organizational behavior that would have the most profound impact on our company's performance, and this behavior was "accountability." We provided our employees with a book entitled, "*QBQ: The Question Behind the Question*" written by John G. Miller. The theme of the book was centered on the concept of "accountability" and provided a process-based approach to improve individual and organizational accountability. To support the teaching materials, we built interactive case studies that enabled our employees to understand the right behaviors associated with accountability, and we used examples to show inappropriate behaviors as well.

Finally, we took one last step that quickly became popular as a lunchroom conversation for employees, and was effective in helping reinforce our values. Shortly after we launched communications regarding our values, about three times a week for one month, I made it a point to go to the lunchroom of the headquarters facility where our main manufacturing operations were located. I carried a handful of lunch coupons that were good for one free lunch. As I greeted employees, I'd ask them if they could name the company values.

On the first day of my lunch tour, the best people could do is provide me with one or two of our four company values, which at the time were Respect, Reliability, Innovation, and Integrity. If they were unable to name these four values, the lunch coupons remained in my pocket. However, before moving on to ask other employees, I provided the correct answers to those people unable to list the values. I promised to ask them what the values were again another day.

After two or three times walking through the lunchroom, employees began to seek me out to ask if I wanted to know the values of the company. Each time they were able to answer correctly, they received a free lunch coupon. And yes, I sought out those people who had not gotten the values right the first time to give them another opportunity. Almost every time, employees knew the values the second time around.

In less than a month, our values were well known throughout the main location of the business, and we took similar actions to spread them to other locations worldwide.

Several months later, we took another step to help our employees better understand and appreciate the company they worked for. Historically, Markem had been a quietly successful company, humble, and understated. Some members of senior management may have been a bit skeptical when I first approached them with the idea to apply for "Best Company to Work For in New Hampshire." The idea of actually bidding for recognition was not the company's style or personality, and we didn't normally seek out this kind of public image. Markem was already well respected in the Keene community as a great company to work for, but it was lesser known in larger cities in New Hampshire like Manchester and Nashua, cities closer to Boston.

Times were changing though and there was present day value in applying for this award. As I presented the idea to some of the senior members of management, I explained that the purpose of our participation in entering the contest wouldn't be for name recognition or recruiting purposes. Instead, our aim was to establish Markem as a great place to work inside our corridors, and to ensure a high level of morale and motivation within our workforce.

In mid-2003, approximately 6-9 months following our initial re-launch of our company values, and within a few weeks of having submitted an application for "Best Company to Work For in New Hampshire," we received a phone call informing us that we were one of 10 finalists in the large-company category of the competition. We were thrilled to hear the news, but it was too soon to celebrate. The head judge informed us that the next stage of the competition would include site visits to each of the finalist companies by a panel of judges. Each visit would include a short introductory meeting with senior executives, a site tour, and the opportunity for judges to meet with employees. He then told us that of ten finalists, five would be named as Best Companies in rank order from one to five.

The day arrived when the panel of judges visited Markem. The panel consisted of various executives and business consultants from different parts of the state, all interested in learning more about Markem's business, internal culture, and work environment. Following executive interviews and a company tour, the judges met with a group of about 15 employees for a 90-minute discussion. At the conclusion of their visit, the judges remarked that they were most impressed by how engaged our employees seemed to be, and how proud they were to work at Markem. Obviously, those of us who heard these words were very pleased, not only because the judges considered their visit a successful one, but also because it was a milestone for us, taking into account how poor the morale of our workforce had been a year or so earlier. The workforce had understood the importance of living our renewed values and taking on the performance challenge that was necessary for us to remain viable and successful. Evidence of this success was reflected in the company's financial performance.

What were the results of the "Best Company to Work For in New Hampshire" competition that year?

Well, in early September we received another phone call from the folks that ran the contest. This time it was to inform us we'd been selected as the number one "Best Company to Work For in New Hampshire" in the large-company category within the whole competition. The magazine that ran the competition, "*New Hampshire Magazine*," informed us they would be coming to write a story and take photos, and we'd be invited to participate in a celebratory event to be held in a couple of months.

After sharing the good news with a few executives and our board of directors, we discussed the different scenarios to inform our workforce. After all, they were the reason we won. While we had expected to do well in the competition, in truth, being selected as the top company in the state was beyond what we'd anticipated. We seized upon the opportunity to celebrate. It became a tremendous boost to our ability to motivate and inspire our workforce, and to build on our momentum in achieving our organizational goals and business strategy.

During this same period, Markem introduced lean management into our operations, updated a new three-year business strategy, and achieved solid financial results. There's no doubt that the efforts to leverage our values and culture by linking them to concrete activities made a meaningful difference for us in our competitive market position and financial results. Likewise, our internal employment brand and external market brand were both strengthened, as our employees successfully carried our values externally to our customers.

We conducted the human capital survey as well, and this feedback mechanism gave us an excellent opportunity to ensure that our workforce and management were on the same page. It was a great way to assess areas where management could improve in engaging our employees more effectively.

During this period Markem received its largest long-term order of equipment and supplies in the history of the company up to that date. According to a high-level Markem sales executive, the customer's management indicated the main reason Markem was selected over the other bidding competitors was the company's ability to bring people from different customer-facing and back office functions together to work seamlessly as a fully functioning team. As you would expect, we used this story repeatedly with our workforce to reinforce the importance our values and culture played in our success.

The above story shows how instrumental an organization's values and culture can be in determining its success. **All of the actions taken to develop an organization's values and culture are based on tangible activities, programs, policies, communications, and processes. The soft words that people often use to describe culture are typically the consequences of these actions.**

Chapter 8
Transforming Business Strategy into Human Capital Initiatives

While I'm not an expert on "business strategy," as a senior executive and participant in many business strategy sessions, I've gained a perspective on what companies do right and wrong in implementing their strategies. However, this book is about Human Capital Management, not business strategy. For this reason, I will only address business strategy as it relates to the business foundation and to goal setting. For those who would like more detail about the specific topic of business strategy, check out one of my favorite books, called *"Leading the Revolution"* by Gary Hamel, the well-known marketing and strategic development guru. Hamel takes a non-traditional approach by challenging companies to reinvent themselves as a way to remain viable. His consulting company, Strategos, is a good choice if you're looking for assistance from a leading-edge company on the topic of business strategy development.

Too many organizations start their strategic renewal process, whether annually or every three years, by jumping directly into "business strategy" without preparation. It's somewhat predictable that this is the case since many CEOs are anxious about how they will generate new sources of revenue and improve their product portfolios through innovation. Many organizations start by completing extensive customer evaluations to determine whether and how much the company is meeting the needs of its customers. Another starting point for organizations is completion of a SWOT analysis, where the company reviews its Strengths, Weaknesses, Opportunities, and Threats, either independently, or in coordination with a customer survey.

In the pre-Internet days, companies used to launch a strategic renewal process every three years or so. Then the pace of technology, globalization, and other competitive factors pushed organizations to initiate annual or rolling three-year strategic renewal processes.

This trend to address business strategy more frequently is a by-product of the speed and probability of change, and with it comes the need to revisit all of the elements of the Human Capital Management System, starting with the business foundation. The business strategy must be a by-product of the business foundation, and alignment between the two is critical to getting the business strategy right. This link between the business foundation and business strategy was first introduced as Figure 1 on page 24, and is shown again below as Figure 6.

Figure 6

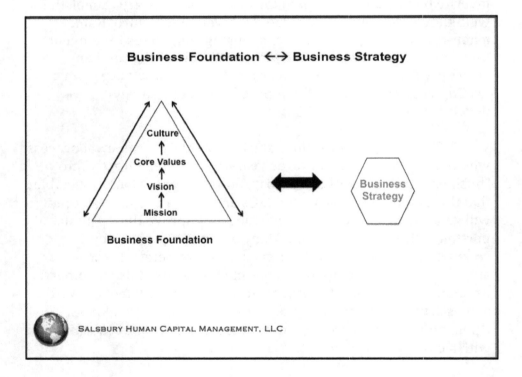

For the purpose of gaining clarity prior to examining the relationship between business strategy and organizational goals, let's first check on the definition of business strategy, as provided by Rapid Business Intelligence Success:

"...business strategy is a long term plan of action designed to achieve a particular goal or set of goals or objectives. Strategy is management's game plan for strengthening the performance of the enterprise." [15]

After the business strategy has been shaped, the next step in the implementation of the Human Capital Management System is the identification of organizational goals. Figure 7 below shows a basic illustration and well-known approach in the process steps of business strategy and goal setting. As shown in the diagram, business strategy comes before goal setting.

Figure 7

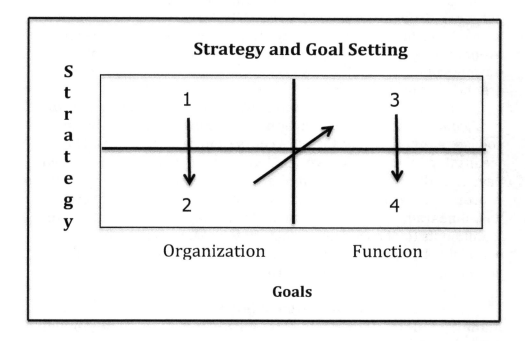

The development of business strategy should be a cross-functional activity. This is the best way to ensure that all of the organization's business functions have visibility to the complete picture. This cross-functional collaboration will generate the most comprehensive business strategy, and it will also encourage buy-in among key senior managers. Finally, cross-functional participation will enable senior management of each function to better understand the key issues and goal requirements that other functions face. The end result should be a business strategy that specifies a number of key mid/long-term strategic goals following the organization's mission and contributing to pursuit of its vision.

Let's take the example of the dilemma faced by most universities in today's Internet-based environment. University administrators know that for the post-secondary educational system, Internet based or online courses are a "strategic inflection point," a term coined by Andy Grove, the former CEO of Intel, and author of *"Only the Paranoid Survive."* The term refers to the point in time when a business must revisit its strategy due to an enormous event or action that will significantly impact the environment the business operates in. Obvious examples of strategic inflection points are the start of the Internet or the occurrence of "9/11."

For most colleges and universities, online learning is and will be a game-changer. It's no longer necessary for students to be on a college campus in order to take a course and receive credits. This means that in order to thrive, let alone survive, most universities will have to address this inflection point in their strategic development process. A typical commitment a university might make is to create an online training curriculum in fields of study that will enable it to maintain its total enrollment. This strategic statement is not actionable by itself, but it's clear enough for a university to formulate actionable organizational goals from it.

Following the formation of business strategy, the senior management team needs to collaborate and agree to high-level organizational goals from the strategy. Some companies make the mistake of establishing functional goals immediately after articulating the organizational business strategy. This may put functional goals in conflict with one another. The determination

of functional goals should only come after organizational goals have been developed.

I can't tell you how many times I've seen the Marketing and Sales functions with conflicting goals because both worked on their own strategy and goals without fully considering the strategy and goals of the other function. This happens between Engineering and Manufacturing as well because they often have goals that may not naturally fit with one another's interests. A common example of a natural conflict between Engineering and Manufacturing is in regards to product design. Typically the Engineering function has responsibility to write engineering specifications, but Manufacturing has to make the product in a cost effective manner. While Engineering's product engineering specifications may include a part that perfectly meets the requirement, it might be too expensive from a manufacturing point of view. The Manufacturing function may find a cheaper part that meets the need, but not to the quality expectations of Engineering. Without clarity regarding quality versus cost as a priority, these types of internal conflicts get in the way of organizational goals being achieved. Since this happens even for those organizations that do a great job of strategy and goal setting, you can imagine how disruptive it can be for organizations doing a poor job rolling out business strategy and organizational goals.

When all the business functions are added into the picture, it's easy to understand how complicated and disjointed an organization can become when each of its functional units have goals that aren't synchronized with the other functions of the organization.

The Balanced Scorecard, introduced by Robert Kaplan and David Norton ("*The Balanced Scorecard – Measures That Drive Performance*," Harvard Business Review, Robert S. Kaplan and David P Norton, January-February 1992) has become popular over the last dozen years in providing an approach to translate organizational strategy into goals. The model does a good job in helping organizations link key organizational goals to the organization's business strategy. The Balanced Scorecard advocates goal setting by looking through four lenses including financial, customer (external), operations (internal), and learning and growth.

These four perspectives are good choices for companies to concentrate their attention in order to ensure that there's a balance between financial and non-financial indicators, and between leading and lagging indicators of performance. However, without careful and disciplined management, implementation of the Balanced Scorecard can result in too many top level goals, or too many functional goals, as each function may feel compelled to add goals and measures for each of the four perspectives (financial, customer, operations, and learning and growth). Also, as goals are cascaded downward in the organization, it can become more difficult for sub-functions or individuals to make a direct link to the higher-level goals at the organizational or functional level. Despite these challenges, the Balanced Scorecard approach is one of the best models available to translate strategic initiatives into goal setting.

Once the business strategy has been defined and organizational goals have been established, their linkage to the business foundation should be reviewed. Many companies spend a tremendous amount of energy translating business strategy into organizational goals, but they don't take the time to do "reverse alignment," that is, to ensure the goals are consistent with the business foundation. This process can be seen in Figure 8 on page 61 where the double-arrows in the diagram show the importance of this principle at each step in the process.

Figure 8

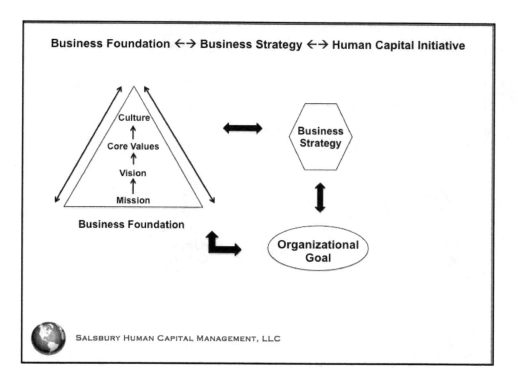

Some people might argue it's enough to ensure that the business strategy is aligned with the business foundation, but misalignment sometimes occurs in the translation of business strategy to organizational goals. Let's look at a diagram that shows an organization seeking to launch an organizational initiative to improve its "performance culture" as a key feature of its business strategy. This is shown in Figure 9 on the page 62.

Figure 9

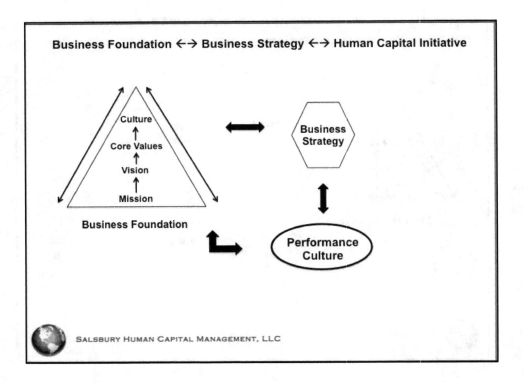

As you can see from Figure 9, "performance culture" has been placed in the box that was formerly represented by "organizational goal" in Figure 8. Note that there are dual arrows connecting the business foundation and business strategy, as well as business strategy and performance culture, and from performance culture back to the business foundation. This dual arrow is intended to highlight the need for each of these system elements to be checked for alignment, and to ultimately test whether the performance goal selected will actively support the mission, vision, values, and culture of the organization. If organizational goals support the business strategy and business foundation, then individual goals can be established to support the organizational goals.

If, on the other hand, organizational goals don't support the business strategy or business foundation, either the organizational goal needs to be modified or the business strategy or business foundation need to be revisited to understand why there is a disconnect. In exceptional circumstances, the business environment may have changed substantially enough to require a modification of the business foundation so that it aligns more closely with the business strategy and organizational goals. If an organization needs to modify its culture in order to survive as an entity, it may need to revisit its business foundation.

Take the case of Kodak, a company that has had numerous business challenges in the recent past, and was cleared to emerge from bankruptcy in late August 2013 after filing a plan for reorganization. In the summer of 2012, I found this mission statement on Kodak's website:

"Upholding the Kodak Mission"

"...we plan to grow more rapidly than our competitors by providing customers with the solutions they need to capture, store, process, output and communicate images, anywhere, anytime. We will derive our competitive advantage by delivering differentiated, cost-effective solutions, including consumables, hardware, software, systems and services, quickly and with flawless quality. All this is thanks to our diverse team of energetic, results-oriented employees with the world-class talent and skills necessary to sustain Kodak as the world leader in imaging." [16]

It's been widely reported in the press that for Kodak to survive and recover, it needs to defocus in many areas, and be more concentrated in its efforts to produce a limited, but relevant range of products and services. Kodak itself announced in 2012 that it would phase out of its dedicated capture device business, and concentrate on online and retail-based photo printing, and desktop inkjet printing. With these changes in business strategy, Kodak has made and will need to make difficult decisions in the future to remain viable.

Further, the company will need to decide how to position itself as it streamlines its product strategy. It will need to address new challenges where speed and quality will be fundamental operational requirements, and this in turn, may require adjustments to the company's culture.

Despite Kodak's recognition that its entire business model must be refashioned, the company's mission statement hasn't been modified. In fact, it's written as if the company will continue to maintain a diverse and comprehensive product portfolio. As a result, it appears that Kodak's business strategy no longer matches its stated mission. Kodak's mission statement is so broad and complex in its description that it would be a challenge for most people to even remember.

Rather than change the strategy and leave the mission statement as is, Kodak would be better served by updating the mission statement and the business strategy so that they're more effectively aligned, current, and easy to understand.

The point is this: the mission statement is the starting point for any company to describe what they're trying to achieve at the present time. If a company is going to take the time to write a mission statement and communicate it to its employees, it must start with a realistic view of who it is and what business it's in. This is especially true when the company's business model has been made obsolete, whether through internal mistakes or external market conditions.

Time will tell if Kodak can rekindle the special qualities that made it such a strong and unique enterprise of the past, but ensuring that its mission and vision are contemporary and realistic according to today's challenges might be a good start for them to establish internal alignment.

The four components of the business foundation are put in place to maintain consistency and to set a standard for the organization with respect to establishing direction and behavior. As noted in the Kodak case, one would expect the mission and vision to be changed only when there are major shifts in the competitive environment, business markets or economy.

Changing values and organizational culture too frequently or not at all when change is drastically needed creates an atmosphere of doubt and dissatisfaction among employees who lose trust and confidence in management. Keeping this in mind, shifts in business strategy or organizational goals that may conflict with the business foundation should be carefully considered.

Values and culture must be consistently managed to properly influence human behaviors and to enable the organization to leverage its human capital with speed and force. Keep in mind that tangible activities and processes are what reinforce a company's culture. This means programs selected to support organizational goals need to be reviewed carefully to ensure that the results will reflect what the organization has intended for its company culture. Equally important, steps need to be taken to prepare for communications with the workforce reinforcing the goals and culture. As you would expect, this step is critical for the Human Capital Management System to function as intended.

Each business function is ready to start work on its functional strategy only after organizational strategy and organizational goals have been developed. My experience shows that companies who do the best job setting strategy and goals are those where the senior leadership of the organization, represented by its functional department heads, work together on the organizational strategy, and then discuss, debate, and decide as a team what each function's strategy should be. This cross-functional collaboration is the best way to ensure each function's strategy is placed appropriately within the overall business strategy, and the functional strategies and goals don't conflict with one another.

Even though a senior functional leader may have already solicited input from functional subordinates prior to strategic planning sessions with the senior leadership team, it's useful to regroup with key functional subordinates after the senior leadership team has vetted functional strategies and goals.

The "top-down" approach to functional strategy and goal setting should naturally flow from the top in determining organizational priorities, but input should also come from the "bottom-up" too. Functional experts or specialists often have insights that should be taken into consideration and may be overlooked by senior members of the organization in strategy or team goal setting.

With the opportunity to utilize a "top-down" approach to goal setting, functional managers should validate or test these functional goals with key members of their team. This will help gain consensus by encouraging participation through feedback in functional strategy and goal setting.

Now that we've reviewed the business foundation and its association with the business strategy and organizational goals, the next section of the book will cover the implementation of key human capital goals or initiatives that are derived from the business strategy.

Section 3
Powering Up the Human Capital Management System

Up until now, you've been introduced to the concept of Human Capital Management as a practice, with an overview of what the Human Capital Management System is, and its potential benefits if rooted properly. You've also become acquainted with the key ingredients of the business foundation, the first phase of the Human Capital Management System. In reviewing the business foundation, we've seen the vital links between building a business foundation and a business strategy, and how to convert a business strategy into action through organizational goals.

Now we'll cover another important element of the Human Capital Management System, the "Human Capital Management Wheel."

Chapter 9
The "Performance Wheel:"
Making the System Go

The "Human Capital Management Wheel," shown below in Figure 10 is the operational driver of the Human Capital Management System. For this reason, I refer to it as the "performance wheel." It includes a set of integrated components or "spokes" that together deliver action-oriented programs and activities supporting the organization's strategy and goals. When combined as components of a system, the action-oriented spokes of the wheel propel a designated human capital initiative that holds the spokes together. These spokes line up with one another, and each program and activity related to a spoke is always developed in consideration of the other spokes.

Figure 10

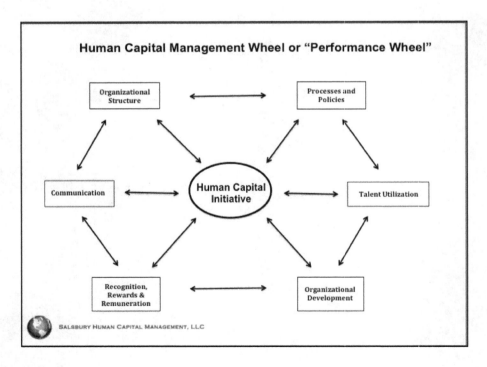

Selection of Initiatives and Supporting Actions are Key Decisions

Typically, "human capital initiatives" within the Human Capital Management System are strategic, not tactical. As a system, all of the components of the performance wheel need to be working in congruence and in support of the human capital initiative in order to achieve maximum results.

As described in Section 1, human capital initiatives are large-scale goals or objectives an organization chooses to pursue that are heavily dependent and reliant on the people of the organization. With this definition in mind, I will refer to "human capital initiatives" going forward as "HCIs." Figure 11 below provides a sample of organizational goals that would be suitable as HCI's.

Figure 11

A Sample of Human Capital Initiatives

Improve Performance Culture

Lean Management
Six Sigma

Integration of an Acquisition or Merger

Build a Global Mindset

Global Talent Acquisition/Management

New Business Model (often including re-organizations)

Re-engineer a functional discipline (Sales, Marketing, etc.)

 SALSBURY HUMAN CAPITAL MANAGEMENT, LLC

The repeated success of human capital initiatives over time leads to the workforce becoming a tangible asset of the organization. This people asset is a competitive weapon to be leveraged.

Most organizations don't strategically plan for the proper execution of HCIs in a comprehensive manner or with a view to integrating the components of the performance wheel. At best, this is a lost opportunity to build momentum within the organization. Unfortunately, companies often pursue HCIs on an individual basis or tactically by proceeding with one-shot programs, rather than utilizing all the spokes of the performance wheel as an integrated unit.

Let's take the earlier example of an organization choosing to improve its performance culture as a primary HCI. In this case, it's unlikely that an isolated activity or program will impact the performance culture radically for the change to be meaningful and long lasting. **For the performance culture to be dramatically changed and endure over the long-term, interdependent actions must be taken so that each of the spokes within the performance wheel work together. These actions can be specific goals or objectives that will directly impact the realization of the HCI itself. They can also be supporting or secondary actions that complement and reinforce the HCI.**

Not all of the elements or actions of the Human Capital Management System need to be (or can be) started simultaneously or at the same pace. The planning of large-scale HCIs should be carefully laid out. Trying to do too much or poor timing enacting a series of actions can have a negative impact. In large-scale endeavors, it may be more beneficial to develop and complete one action or program at a time to attain short-term and incremental results, as opposed to tackling multiple projects where resources will be spread thin, and results won't be seen for an extended period of time.

This is well known by "solutions" companies, many who've learned through trial and error that more traction can be gained by first completing individual products or services before trying to build a complete solution. Building a complete solution can take too much time and sales opportunities are lost while competitors are selling individual products or services, taking market share, and establishing market leadership. Therefore, in general it's easier to be successful with a large-scale human capital project when there are already one or more key actions or programs in place as a baseline.

Let's take the case of IBM's transformation into a solutions company from a hardware company. IBM couldn't have made the transition from a mainframe computer company to a software solutions company if it hadn't already had a long history of selling products and services that allowed it to climb up the value chain. IBM had a baseline of knowledge that was critical for them to integrate the different components of their solution.

The same could be said for Apple Computer. Their ability to effectively integrate hardware, software, and the operating system together was the foundation to building multiple products from the MacBook, to the iPod, to the iPad.

Developing and preparing for a major organizational initiative and connecting all the elements of an organizational system are much like developing a solutions business. Several new initiatives can't all be executed at one time when there are monetary, resource, and time constraints. **Determining which HCI to choose as the primary centerpiece of the performance wheel is an important decision if an organization is to maximize its ability to transform its human capital into a competitive advantage. When following this step, it's imperative to select the right programs and activities to support each spoke of the performance wheel.**

Companies choosing the wrong initiative or programs to support the initiative typically make one of three mistakes:

1) **They don't select the appropriate initiative for the centerpiece of the performance wheel.** They may incorrectly choose an HCI that won't give the organization the desired cause-and-effect relationship to support the business strategy or organizational goals they're wishing to fulfill.

2) **Companies sometimes choose a single program as the performance wheel centerpiece, when the program should've been a secondary action supporting one of the**

performance wheel spokes. For example, many organizations establish succession planning as a tool to help build a talent management system. In doing so, succession planning becomes the centerpiece of the performance wheel, when in reality the development of a talent management system should be the centerpiece. Succession planning is more fitting as a program supporting the "organizational development" spoke of the performance wheel.

3) **Companies often choose the wrong programs or actions to support their HCI.** This happens for any number of reasons, but the most likely reasons are the following:

• Individuals in leadership positions don't have the experience to recognize which specific programs should be developed to support the selected HCI.

• Programs or actions of one spoke within the performance wheel aren't complementary to programs or actions of other spokes. In some cases they even conflict with one another. One of the most common examples of this that I've seen in my career are those companies who implement succession planning programs, but also use mid-career hiring strategies, rather than hiring and training entry-level cadre. This prevents the development of a feeder system that is typically required for an effective "promote-from-within" system to become established. For an HCI to be far-reaching and capable of having a major impact on an organization, it has to have an integrated and system-based impact, where actions supporting each performance wheel spoke complement each other.

• A program becomes ineffective if it's designed incorrectly. This may occur simply because of poor execution or it may occur as a result of little or no thought given to the relationship and correlation between the different elements of the Human Capital Management System. There should always be a direct link from the business foundation to the business strategy to the HCI to the performance wheel spoke/component and finally to the action or programs to drive the initiative.

- Companies often choose the wrong programs or activities of a performance wheel spoke to implement first. Rather than choosing "high impact-low organizational investment" actions, they focus on efforts that don't generate the organizational energy needed.

- Finally, they try and accomplish too much at once, slowing down meaningful progress toward ultimate transformation of human capital as a competitive advantage.

Both the primary HCI and the programs/actions of the spokes need to be capable of generating enthusiasm and making visible progress for the organization to see.

This is particularly important when selecting large-scale initiatives that will take a long time to complete. Under these circumstances, it's best for multiple actions to be phased in over time.

In some cases it will be readily apparent to an organization which HCI they should start with first. An organization's needs may be so specific or essential to the business strategy that it's clear what the HCI and related actions should be. In many other cases though, the selection of HCIs or supporting actions aren't clear at first.

If the selection of an HCI or supporting program isn't apparent, senior management should think about building a "strategic human capital action plan." This type of plan is similar to a strategic business plan, except its emphasis is specific to human capital. When building such a plan, the following basic questions should get you started:

- What HCI or program will generate the greatest positive impact on the organization's human capital performance? What is the timeline needed to accomplish this?

- What HCI or program will generate the quickest wins, and build momentum?

- What HCI will require the most/least time, cost and organizational inertia?

While there are always other questions to be answered, the determination and priority of an HCI and supporting program or actions should be evaluated logically using the following 2x2 decision matrix, shown in Figure 12 below.

Figure 12

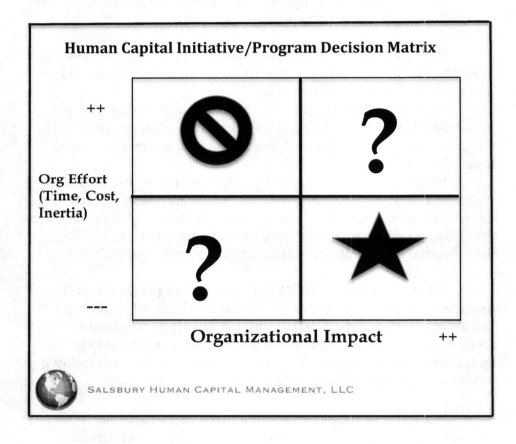

Naturally, like any other organizational goal, the best choice for selection of an HCI is the one with the "greatest benefit for the least amount of time, cost or organizational energy." The star in Figure 12 represents this principle.

The less desirable option is always the one offering the least organizational impact, but requiring the most organizational effort. The other combinations are more challenging to choose from and should be determined based on the specific needs and circumstances of an organization at the present time.

Choosing an initiative with "high organizational impact and high organizational effort" over "low organizational impact and low organizational effort" isn't always the best choice, although it may be tempting to go with the high impact/high effort approach. The right decision for an organization should be based on the urgency to building an organizational impetus, and sometimes a small win in a shorter time period could be most beneficial. On the other hand, a company might want to work on an initiative providing a competitive advantage that's best kept quiet until there is a substantial and tangible result that catches its competitors off guard.

Advance Preparation Generates Organizational Energy

Once an HCI has been selected, its implementation shouldn't be moved forward abruptly without proper planning. There can be a fine line between quick-but-adequate preparation and rushed, inadequate planning that can lead to project failure.

There must always be a commitment to professionally prepare for the launch, and to support the initiative with frequent and consistent actions that will help it take hold organizationally. The senior management team needs to provide clear communications to middle management and the entire workforce so the employee relations' aspect of the initiative is positively received. This will require preliminary communications including marketing and sales messaging activities directed at the workforce. While every CEO would like the organization to follow his/her lead without question, most of the more successful CEO communicators understand that a heavy organizational initiative can only begin when enough work has been done up front to prepare for it. This doesn't mean all aspects of the initiative need to be put in place prior to communicating the initiative, but there is a minimal level of preparation necessary to proceed. In addition, senior management must provide reinforcement through actionable participation from conceptualization to completion.

Far too many times, senior management introduces a new initiative to an organization and then quickly moves on to other business priorities before the initiative has taken hold. Often, this is because senior managers have spent time together discussing the topic in great depth prior to the project being rolled out. By the time the rest of the organization receives the first communication, senior managers have discussed the topic so many times they feel like it's time to move on to the next issue. More often than not, senior management doesn't spend enough time helping the rest of the organization understand the rationale for new initiatives, human capital or otherwise.

To further support this point, vendor organizations offering "employee surveys" will be the first to point out one of the most common criticisms employees have of management is "poor communication." This point was brought home to me personally when contemplating the introduction of the "human capital survey" at Markem Corporation.

When we decided to commence with this survey at Markem in the early 2000's, we were less interested in "employee satisfaction" topics, such as whether people thought they were paid well or whether they liked working at the company. We were more interested in understanding whether our employees understood the relationship between their jobs and the success of the company. In other words, this survey was a "business alignment" survey.

Based on vendor feedback, Markem was in the top 90th percentile of industrial B2B companies in regards to frequency, openness, and quality of communications. Yet, when the results of the human capital survey were collected, "improvement in communication" was cited as one of the three key areas that needed management's attention. With further efforts to analyze the survey results, we learned from employees that it was direct manager-employee communications that was lacking.

This example underscores the importance of ensuring that communications links are established at all levels of the organization effectively. It's senior management's responsibility to ensure that this is happening. If a link in the communications chain is broken, either downward or upward, then the message is lost or diminished. Therefore, the need for active communications at the senior management level and at the manager-employee level is critical.

The buildup and preparation for a project is equally important. One way to accomplish this is to bring additional people into the planning aspect of the human capital project. There are at least three reasons why this is beneficial:

1) Large-scale human capital projects require multiple actions and as a result, "many hands make lighter work." Simply stated, the prep work needing completion can be done faster with more people.

2) Having capable people who can provide insights, feedback, and help mold the key aspects of a project is a good quality control approach. Increasing pre-launch involvement of a limited number of people who can perform the early preparatory work will enhance the quality of the outcome.

3) Every human capital project needs to have champions ready to carry enthusiasm to the project. Waiting until after the announcement and start of a project to enlist and engage champions will create a gap in the process, and require senior management to sell more than necessary. While it's senior management's responsibility to communicate and sell the initiative continuously, having additional champions can have a more transmissible effect in generating organizational motivation and commitment.

These steps don't comprehensively explain the finer points of project management, but they do highlight some key considerations prior to starting an initiative. The effort put forth to comprehensively plan for a Human Capital Management transformation will enhance the chances for success of the HCI and related actions.

Chapter 10
Advantages and Disadvantages of Organizational Structure in Human Capital Management

Organizations should be designed for the primary purpose of achieving their strategies and goals. Management develops policies, processes, and other operational guidelines to support the organizational structure in place. Many times, organizational structures are designed for management control and efficiencies, but there are more benefits to organizational design and structure than these. In companies that practice Human Capital Management, organizational design and structure can be leveraged in a way most organizations haven't thought about.

Let's take the case of IBM. Several years ago, the company found itself as a potentially obsolete and oversized bureaucracy with a mainframe business model that was being overtaken by the proliferation of networked and interconnected computers. Sam Palmisano, then CEO, recognized that in order to satisfy its core base of enterprise clients and survive in the next generation of the computer industry, IBM would need to transform itself into a global service provider optimizing service delivery rather than hardware products. At the time, Palmisano coined the term "Globally Integrated Enterprise" (GIE) to reflect the need that IBM had to become a provider of integrated services and global delivery.

The decision to move from a product and geographically organized business to one delivering nimble and effective enterprise solutions anywhere in the world would be quite a task for any company to manage.

The fact that IBM had a global workforce of over 300,000 only served to magnify the size of the challenge that it faced. In addressing this challenge, leadership at IBM conceptualized the Workforce Management Initiative (WMI), an HCI that became the foundation for the company's development as a globally integrated enterprise.

Like all HCIs, the WMI was multifaceted and included related actions touching on all parts of the organization. Among other efforts, this included updated job descriptions and competencies that could be commonly understood and utilized on a global basis, and as a common language that would enable standardization of job roles and skill sets across international borders. Most impressive of the actions surrounding this initiative was IBM's ability to transform its organizational design and structure operationally. Management and individual contributors bought into the concept of working as globally integrated teams.

This type of transition would be too difficult of a cultural obstacle for many companies to overcome due to the size and significance of the challenge being undertaken. IBM was able to make the transition because it recognized the need for a paradigm change, and made the necessary large-scale business model changes required to transform a company of its size and global reach. IBM's leadership understood that a transition from a products and services company to a solutions company would require a game-changing approach based on the company's business model and organizational design.

IBM's success with WMI is evidenced by its results in nearly every important financial category. Revenue, net income, and earnings per share have all consistently grown over the last several years to record numbers. IBM's ability to globally integrate all of its major enterprise functions from service delivery to marketing resulted in gains of more than $6B in enterprise productivity savings between 2006-2011, while simultaneously improving quality. For more on IBM's transformation and to understand this case study in more detail, check out John W. Boudreau's series of case studies titled *"IBM's Global Talent Management Strategy: The Vision of the Globally Integrated Enterprise,"* 2010, Society for Human Resource Management.

I've found that there's no perfect organizational structure. Each has its strengths and weaknesses, and the trick is to structure the business in a way that best enables the organization for maximum success. In theory, the structure of the organization should be lined up to support the business strategy in view of the organization's business foundation, consisting of the mission, vision, values, and culture.

Every organization has a unique history, business foundation and business strategy. The decision to select one organizational structure over another one requires a company to reflect on where it is in its life cycle, competitive position, as well as operational constraints and advantages.

One type of organizational structure may benefit one part of a company while another type may be more beneficial to another part. For example, a decentralized division of a major corporation may prefer a "product" or "division" based design, with all of the functions supporting the division reporting to the division President. On the other hand, the corporate headquarters group that the division reports to may want its staff functions (Finance, IT, etc.) to manage across all of its divisions, and choose a centralized organizational structure. In this case, the staff functions might report to functional corporate VPs, while the line functions may report to the division President. This kind of structure is very common in large companies as it's more efficient and operationally effective by design.

Many companies don't approach organizational design as professionally and appropriately as they should. Sometimes organizational structures are decided haphazardly and carelessly. On more than one occasion, I've observed an organization's structure determined by one of the following:

- The CEO selected an organizational structure from his/her past experience, without any regard to what makes most sense for the current organization, or

- The CEO chose the organizational structure that provided the most direct management control, or

- A "napkin decision" was made where the CEO and one or two other senior managers figuratively sat in a restaurant and drew the organization structure on a napkin, without adequately vetting other approaches and comparing their strengths and weaknesses.

The determination of an appropriate and effective organizational structure isn't an exact science. There is no direct formula. There are multiple considerations leading to the most appropriate structure, and there are various constituencies who may benefit differently according to the one selected. With this in mind, there are a number of options to think about for choosing the most appropriate organizational structure. The Society of Human Resource Management (SHRM) defines the most common designs as follows:

*"**functional** structures are defined by the services they contribute to the organization's overall mission, such as marketing and sales, operations and HR. In a **product (or division)** organization, functional departments are grouped under major project divisions.*

*A **geographic** structure is very similar to a product structure except that geographic regions, rather than products, define the organizational chart.*

*The **hybrid** structure mixes elements of functional, product and geographic organizations.*

*The **matrix** structure has ties to both product and geographic divisions...an employee...may have two bosses: one from the product side and one from the geographic side."* 17

Other organizational structures can be based on team approaches or networks and are often temporary. In these structures, key positions or functions are grouped together to work cross-functionally on a project.

For the purpose of our review, we'll examine how various organizational structures influence the success or failure of an HCI. **Given that each type of organizational structure has its own strengths and weaknesses, it's important to understand how the strengths can be leveraged, and the weaknesses can be neutralized or diminished.** In comparing different organizational structures, we will assume that the rollout of an initiative within that type of structure will be cascaded down in the organization from top management to middle management and then to individual contributors respectively.

Functional: The functional organization is one of the more simple designs. It's efficient and relatively easy to work with compared to other structures in the execution of organizational goals. The levels of communication to the workforce are fewer. Typically there would be no more than three or four basic layers of communication assuming a "cascading top-down" approach is being employed. That is, the CEO to senior management, senior management to mid-management by function, then functional mid-management to first-line supervision and/or to individual contributors. The strength of having fewer layers is it makes the ease of communication greater, and there's less likelihood that messages will become distorted or misinterpreted as they're passed down. This type of organizational structure brings the CEO closer to rank-and-file employees, and allows for a more direct communication when appropriate.

Assuming the message from the top is the correct one, it's often beneficial for employees to hear directly from the CEO so that important messages have the desired effect and impact. Hearing from the CEO rather than from functional management can be more motivating. Think of how much more inspiring it would be for you to hear from the head of your company about a key topic.

However, organizations need to be careful in overusing the CEO to communicate. If other senior level functional managers aren't actively involved, they may not take an appropriate level of accountability when problems arise, and the initiative will lose steam.

As the breadth and depth of organizations grow, especially globally, the weaknesses of functional organization structures in rolling out corporate wide HCIs are more apparent. This happens for a number of reasons, including the challenge of building efficient, real-time communications for multiple countries and time zones.

The cultural nuances of communicating HCIs are extremely important. Functional organizations with global reach need to take extra precautions when communicating and executing global organization-wide initiatives. Translating one language to another can be confusing and in some cases the literal translation has a very different meaning than the one intended.

Ethnocentric organizations have the tendency to expect that messages from headquarters will be understood in the context that they were meant. Some senior managers are culturally insensitive when communicating to employees of other nationalities. Few senior managers have the global mindset to even recognize when they're using words or phrases that will be misunderstood by those working in countries outside their own. Regardless of the reason, this hurts the credibility of the person relaying the message and damages company communications.

Unfortunately, American led organizations tend to be particularly insensitive to cross-cultural communications. It's uncommon for them to test or be on the lookout for language issues. Many turn to the excuse that English is accepted as the internationally recognized business language. Whatever the reason, it's very uncommon for American companies to put important global communications through cultural and language scans prior to releasing them, and this can result in misinterpreted communications.

Another similar problem with global functional communications is that many times they're not conducted face-to-face. Senior managers hold conference calls or webinars with functional subordinates who are dispersed globally, and while practical, these can diminish the quality of the communication that takes place. They may also decrease the effectiveness of subsequent communications or actions taken by mid-level overseas managers who must relay these messages to their subordinates.

Product: The product organization structure typically provides for separate divisions with their own profit and loss responsibility. Functional roles report to the division President, who reports to the headquarters organization. From a divisional operating point of view, the product organization is the preferred structure since everyone on the team is seeking to achieve the goals of the division.

With that said, this type of organization is less efficient than the functional organization because staff functions such as Finance and HR are duplicated when there are multiple divisions. Additionally, unless headquarters builds formal bridges across the divisions, there's no natural way for the divisions to share technology or best practices. Globally structured product organizations can have the same kind of problem as functional organizations. Despite the fact that employees in a product organization work for the same division, messages become diluted when they're transferred from the division headquarters to other countries.

When it comes to putting HCIs into action, product structures are more complicated than functional structures. Headquarters initiatives are especially complicated, as they require an additional layer of communication. To be effective, the division CEO and his/her senior management team must support HQ initiatives. The handover from "corporate to division" must be completed comprehensively and professionally as well. I've seen numerous initiatives fail miserably because headquarters personnel did a poor job preparing the divisions for the rollout, or provided little direction for support or follow-up. I've seen just as many initiatives fail as a result of division leadership not viewing the headquarters initiative as a critical element of the division strategy. While lip service or minimal effort was made to satisfy corporate management, not much was done to support it at the divisional level.

Geographic: The chief of each region or country reports to the headquarters CEO in geographic organizations. Geographic structures can be very effective when there is significant critical mass in each region. This enables an organization to proactively drive regional and local markets outside of the headquarters country.

In geographic organizations, messages from headquarters often become ineffectively communicated due to inadequate translation or transfer from headquarters to the regions or countries. Geographic organizations are well placed to influence global messages and initiatives since senior managers within the regions participate as members of the executive team that reports to the headquarters' CEO. Since they're usually part of discussions early in an initiative's development process, they can point out cultural or language issues that may exist.

Geographic structures have a similar disadvantage as product organizations since geographic demands and priorities might compete with HQ priorities. With regions being far away from headquarters, and with region leaders concentrated on regional goals, HQ initiatives may not get the attention desired by HQ. In some cases, companies organized by geography can be so decentralized that the regions develop their own company values, culture, and strategy. When this occurs, the geographic organizational model is not only ineffective in support of HQ initiatives, but it's also an organization working contrary to its overall purpose.

Hybrid or Matrix: Sometimes the determination of organization structure is simplified by the size of the organization, its geographic footprint or the extensiveness of its product range. In general, the less complex an organization is, the more likely that a functional, product or geographic organizational structure may be suitable.

Let's face it. Most for-profit companies (and many not-for-profit) are in the business of "growth for survival," and as such, they attempt to grow their business by adding size, new geographies, and/or new products. For this reason, organizational structures may need to be changed as companies change in size and scope.

As organizations become more complex, the mix of functional, product and/or geographic structures become more prevalent. This approach is known as a "hybrid" structure. When these structures result in dual reporting relationships for managers, the hybrid structure becomes a "matrix" structure. Hybrid and matrix organization structures are effective when roles and responsibilities are well defined and coordinated. In general though, the more complex the organization is, the more complex the rollout of the HCI will be. The more complex the rollout becomes, the more chances there are for failure. That's why it's important to understand the built-in strengths and weaknesses of organizational design relative to human capital initiatives.

How to Neutralize Organizational Structure in Completing Human Capital Initiatives

When making decisions about executing HCIs, managers should compare the advantages and disadvantages of the organizational structure in place. In particular, the weaknesses of the organization's design need to be neutralized or reduced, and the strengths enhanced. Here are a number of relevant organizational design questions and comments to reflect on prior to the development and enactment of HCIs:

- Identify the current organizational structure within your organization. What are the inherent strengths and weaknesses of the structure relative to the HCI?

- When looking at these pluses and minuses, what is likely to be the best process approach to commence with the HCI across the organization? Should a "top-down" approach be employed or should management make use of an alternative method?

- What actions will highlight and take advantage of the strengths of the organizational structure in the implementation of the initiative, and how will the weaknesses or obstacles be neutralized or countered?

- Who in the senior management team should be the champion of the initiative? Who or what are the most likely road blockers or skeptics? It can be helpful to invite skeptics to play a role in advance preparation. This is the best way to sway or neutralize them. In some cases, skeptics not fully convinced of an initiative's importance may directly or indirectly sabotage it before it gets off the ground. Keeping this in mind it's essential to deal with questions and concerns at the earliest opportunity.

- Determine what specific role(s) the CEO will play in the initiative. It's important for it not to interfere with the responsibility that should reside with his/her management team. For example, in a geographic structure would it be better for the CEO to communicate to the Asia senior management team or would it be more effective if the executive of the Asia management team were to own the communication? If the CEO communicates directly to the Asia management team, will this undermine the authority and credibility of the Asia VP? The correct answer depends partially on whether or not the Asia VP can effectively communicate the message in a way the CEO would like it to be delivered.

- The most difficult initiatives to accomplish are those HQ unilaterally delivers without first engaging and soliciting buy-in or feedback from product or geographic management teams. Product and geographic organizations usually have their own P&L's, and by nature regard HQ to be intrusive. This is particularly true with large conglomerates having subsidiaries or divisions operating independently. To complicate matters, there's a tendency for executives in staff positions at the corporate level to drive programs that justify their existence, but these programs may not be valued at the division level. When these programs are passed to the division from HQ, sometimes they aren't welcomed enthusiastically. There may be pushback from division management to HQ when there are too many corporate programs and initiatives coming from headquarters.

- The best way to overcome a lack of support for any initiative is by encouraging involvement. In a company organized by products, it's beneficial to engage key people within each of the product groups to participate in the development of the initiative. This is valuable because product divisions will accept the initiative more readily.

- Thought should be given to building "bridge" steps for enactment of HCIs. What I mean by a "bridge step" is the transfer of responsibility that takes place between one part of the organization and another during the deployment of an HCI. For example, let's say a corporation has decided to initiate "leadership competencies" globally. HQ is sponsoring the program and the initial communication and training will take place with the Presidents of each of the divisions reporting to HQ. The first bridge step is the transfer of information regarding the leadership competencies from HQ to the Presidents. How will this take place and who is involved? Chances are that the hand-off to this group of executives will be more successful if some or all of them are involved in the development of the leadership competencies. Another bridge step in this example is the transfer of the leadership competencies to the next level of management within each of the divisions. How will this be accomplished and who will do it? It's imperative in the planning process of the HCI to determine each "bridge step," how organizational assets can be most effectively put to use, and what barriers need to be overcome.

Here are a few additional hints regarding the relationship between organizational structure and the rollout of HCIs:

- Ensure that people driving the initiative have the capability to work cross-functionally, cross-geographically and cross-organizationally. If the operational manager of the initiative is from HQ, he/she must have the capability to understand the subtleties of driving initiatives into divisions or organizations that don't necessarily want them.

- Overcome the obvious weaknesses of the organizational structure as they relate to the establishment of initiatives. For example, understanding that product or division structures are naturally more resistant to HQ driven initiatives, include key individuals from these divisions in the development phase of the initiative. Then, make sure they report back to their organizations to keep key executives informed and updated as the initiative takes shape and gains traction.

- In global organizations, ensure that language and cultural nuances have been fully vetted. While it's impractical to have

people from every global location offer their critiques and
language/cultural edits, it is advantageous to have the
assistance of 2-3 key non-HQ language/culture ambassadors
to offer feedback prior to getting underway.

- Ensure at each "bridge step" that the messages and content of
the initiatives are well understood and aptly communicated
by those delivering them. Build in feedback mechanisms to be
sure the messages have been delivered as they were
envisioned. This is significant since large-scale initiatives are
often cascaded into the organization by an increasing number
of people as the initiative goes deeper into the organization.

Location Choice as a Component of Organizational Design

One type of organizational design that hasn't been covered
yet is "location." By location, I am referring to an organization's
physical locations relative to the organizational design. Location
choices should be tied directly to the overall business strategy.
Organizational structure usually isn't something a company would
change to accommodate an HCI.

However, there are occasions when such changes do make
sense. One example that comes to mind is a company that moved its
headquarters office from Boston to Orlando. At the time, company
executives were as geographically dispersed as the companies they
represented. Group Presidents (positions that managed a group of
companies and reported to the CEO of the corporation) and their
staffs were advised that they would be expected to move to Orlando.
Additionally, a handful of new senior level staff positions were
created and filled in Orlando, and it became very clear management
was serious about changing the way it operated internally as a
corporation.

These actions came as a result of the CEO's push to move the
company from a decentralized conglomerate of mostly disconnected
companies to a more integrated corporation intent on improving its
operational efficiencies. Concurrently, the CEO wanted the divisions
to maintain an entrepreneurial spirit and ownership of their
customers.

The CEO's expectation of executives from Group jobs to move to Orlando sent a strong message throughout the corporation and especially to senior executives about teamwork and economies of scale. This was to be a major cultural change in the way that the company would operate going forward.

During the next few years, the company's culture was indeed modified to this hybrid organizational design approach, combining the best attributes of decentralization (entrepreneurship, accountability, customer ownership, etc.) and centralization (buying efficiencies, cross fertilization of talent, etc.). This is only one example of the systems-based approach applied to modify the company's culture, but it's one showing how organizational structure and location play a key role at the center of the HCI.

Frequent Changes in Organizational Design are Problematic

I've been amazed throughout my career at how many times a change in leadership brings about a change in organizational structure. No sooner does a new CEO become appointed, and within 6-12 months a new organizational structure is announced. Could it really be that the previous organizational structure was incorrect to begin with or was execution the problem?

It's not my intent to suggest that only new CEOs make organizational structure changes. Incumbent CEOs also make organizational structure changes. Surprisingly though, many CEOs don't appreciate how much organizational stress and energy comes with organizational structural changes. For those senior managers in place during the previous CEO's administration, they need to explain why the new organizational structure will be better than the previous structure. This can be a challenge when an organizational structure being replaced was only operational for 2-3 years, and employees were under the prior impression that the previous structure was appropriate at the time. The net result of organizational structure changes is often organizational uncertainty and skepticism.

With organizational design and structural changes, clear communication is needed to explain why the change is being made (usually incorporating some reason as to why the previous structure was not appropriate for the future). Roles need to be redefined and operating processes need to be changed. An organization that goes

from being product structured to geographically structured will
need to redefine its product-to-market process from
conceptualization to product launch. The actions and process
required to successfully implement an organizational structure
change is by itself a major initiative.

Understanding there is no single organizational structure that
is perfect, the decision to make significant structural changes should
be carefully deliberated. Such changes may make sense when
supported by facts and data showing the current structure doesn't
support the business strategy or when market or business
conditions have changed dramatically. Otherwise, organizational
structure changes can be a waste of time, resources, and
organizational energy.

Consequences of Organizational Design Choices

Most senior managers don't understand the consequences of
their organizational structure. The reason for this is fairly simple:
organization structures are designed to support broad strategic and
overall business goals. They're not usually designed to drive specific
HCIs. As a result, senior managers normally don't link the traits of
the organizational structure with the other spokes/components of
the performance wheel.

Let's take a couple of examples to illustrate this point:

Example 1: The Functional Organization Attempting to Globalize

Company A was originally organized "functionally" with
headquarters in the USA. As a result of strong international growth,
over time the company added engineering and manufacturing
centers in Europe and Asia, and built up regional Sales and Service
structures throughout the world. While the company grew
internationally by sending US expatriates overseas to start and grow
its business, as it grew, it replaced the expats with local managers in
each of its international locations. The company continues to be
functionally organized today, and seeks to build a long-term growth
strategy based on being truly global. Ultimately the company would
like to have a senior management team that reflects its international

footprint.

Despite its dreams to become a global company, Company A has maintained its original US-centric view of compensation, training, and development approaches. As a result, it's had some difficulty in its efforts to globalize its talent pool. The company still makes most decisions from headquarters and hasn't developed an international executive team. US expatriates hold most key leadership positions around the world.

Example 2: The Division Organization Attempting to Leverage its Geographic Strengths

Company B is an American company organized by product, and each division operates independently. With the exception of a few corporate roles linked to legal and board related activities, all of the decisions of each business are made by each of the division management teams. In Division 1 of Company B, 80% of the company's revenue comes from international sources outside the USA. Europe and Asia account for approximately 70% of the division's international revenue. Similarly, Division 1 employs over 2,000 people internationally and has multiple operations with over 50 employees in cities across Europe and Asia.

Division 2 of Company B does most of its business in the USA. Its business strategy includes an emphasis on international growth starting with Asia, but it has limited knowledge or experience in how to operate there. Company B does little to promote contact or facilitate interaction between its divisions.

Regrettably, in each of these examples, neither of these companies is taking the appropriate actions necessary to support their business strategies. The companies are stuck to the original support systems of their organizational structures and don't see the need to make the necessary changes or adaptations in their actions to move forward in support of their growth strategies.

For many companies who see organizational structures for little more than control or efficiency tools, they don't understand that the organizational structure is simply one spoke in the performance wheel. Instead, they mistakenly see their organizational structure as a foundation from which other management tools, processes and actions should flow.

Chapter 11
Processes and Policies:
Working in Tandem

In this chapter, we'll review process and policy management as elements of the Human Capital Management System, with particular attention to their alignment with HCIs. This will include an example showing process and policy management tools that have been effectively used in an organization in which I've worked. Second, we'll briefly examine process management programs that can be HCIs themselves. In closing this chapter, we'll underscore the importance of using processes and policies to support each other, as well as the company's business foundation and HCIs an organization has chosen to pursue.

A Big Picture View of Processes and Policies

A former colleague and I were in a conversation regarding how company cultures are created. "If you want to establish a culture," he said, "it's all about setting up processes and policies. They'll drive the way the company will operate and directly influence the behavior of people in an organization."

For sure, there are other factors influencing an organization's culture. It's not all about process or policy management. Nonetheless, organizational processes and policies do have a significant impact on the development of an organization's culture and working environment.

Many companies utilize process management as the primary operational facilitator of decision-making in the organization. This "process management" mentality can serve companies well as they eliminate waste and improve efficiencies, but if overused, they can create an environment within the organization where "process" becomes more important than "content."

Policy management can also drive organizations, with policies being written for every aspect of the organization's operations. These types of organizations typically flourish where repetition, consistency, and standardization are important. Sometimes, policy management driven organizations are considered bureaucratic because decision-making can become paralyzed by overreliance on policy language when dealing with unorthodox problems.

With that said, some organizational leaders are simply allergic to processes and policies, incorrectly believing that they slow down decision-making, creativity, and bias for action. Managers who are averse to process and policy management often avoid it by claiming that adherence to it will hamper their ability to manage effectively on a real-time basis.

Whether or not you are a believer in process and policy management, most people would agree these management tools can be overused or underused, giving them a bad name in either circumstance. But good process and policy management are key ingredients in a fully functioning organization. Let's take a closer look at process management as a tool in the Human Capital Management System.

Process Management is the "Means to an End"

A business process is commonly understood as a series of activities or steps having an intended result or goal. Every business or business function has processes allowing for consistency and efficiency of operations. Some organizations pursue the highest levels of process management in what has been referred to as Business Process Management (BPM). BPM *"is a management discipline that treats business processes as assets that directly contribute to enterprise performance by driving operational excellence and business agility. As with other assets, determining the right level of investment in the resources needed, proper performance monitoring of the process, sound maintenance of the process and management of the process life cycle can drive operational excellence."*[18]

Business Process Management (BPM) can play a meaningful role as a formal approach to process management. Many BPM proponents place it above other organizational assets, including human capital. **When organizations choose processes over people, ultimately the result is that people are valued less than the processes they manage. Therefore, the conclusion drawn here is that processes should be components of a Human Capital Management System, not the focal point of the system itself.**

There's no reason why an organization can't choose to maximize process management and Human Capital Management simultaneously. They're not mutually exclusive. One way to accomplish this is to assign a process management tool at the center of the performance wheel. There are a number of process management techniques and tools that have become popular in the past several years including six-sigma and lean management. Either of these are suitable candidates as HCIs.

Whatever process management tools are implemented, they shouldn't be regarded as the Holy Grail in bringing value to an organization. **Process management is a means to an end, to be used effectively with other tools. In today's world of "copy exact" and the long list of process tools available, there's much more upside in the utilization of people as a competitive advantage over processes.**

Now let's review an example where a process management tool can be an HCI. In Figure 13 below, "lean management" is the HCI at the center of the performance wheel. In this example, we'll look at lean management's relationship with three of the performance wheel spokes: "organizational structure," "processes and policies," and compensation as a tool of "recognition, rewards, and remuneration."

Figure 13

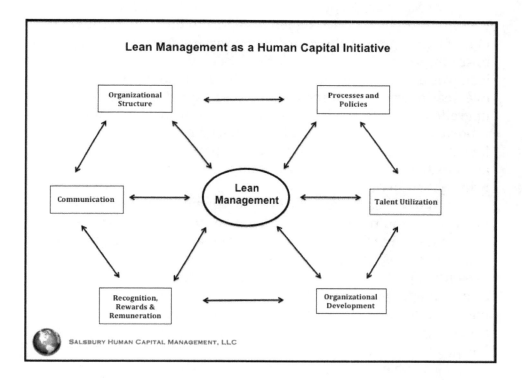

In its simplest form, lean management is a process management tool that reduces waste and builds efficiencies in an organization with the ultimate purpose of maximizing the value provided to the customer. The introduction and implementation of lean management is a major undertaking requiring a systematic approach to be successful, and includes a host of activities and tools to be imbedded in a company's infrastructure and operations. Let's now examine a few of the components of lean management as an HCI.

Many companies embed lean management in their Manufacturing function, which is the most traditional approach. In introducing lean management, it's logical for those managers in charge of lean operations to report to the Manufacturing function. For companies who seek to employ lean across the entire organization, consideration should be given to having lean personnel report to a function independent of the Manufacturing operation of the company.

At Markem Corporation, lean was started in 2003, and a Lean Facilitator was initially assigned to report to the Vice President of Manufacturing Operations for North America. As the company began to see improvements in the metrics associated with its operations, lean was expanded throughout the whole company, including overseas operations. At the time, the position of Lean Facilitator was upgraded to Vice President of Continuous Improvement and reported directly to the President of the company. As you can imagine, this change in structure and reporting had an immediate and positive impact on the importance of lean management as a priority within the company.

The "process and policies" component of the lean management initiative provided a new way for the workforce to look at our internal processes. Instead of viewing a process as a set of steps or actions within a work cell, each process was examined more broadly as part of a value chain through a process called "value stream mapping." This method examines the flow of labor and materials required to deliver a service or product to the customer. In a lean implementation, the value stream mapping methodology is a key process of the HCI.

The objective of lean management is to eliminate waste, drive process improvements, and eliminate excess labor hours. This aspect of lean is challenging to deal with from a human capital point of view. On one hand, lean management attempts to generate enthusiasm within the workforce to find waste and efficiency, and on the other, eliminates jobs as efficiencies occur.

When lean management was introduced at Markem, management sought to actively engage the workforce in embracing lean principles. Employees were encouraged to sign up to participate in kaizen (the Japanese word for improvement) weeklong events where the goal was to drive for efficiency improvements. Yet, they understood pro-active participation in these events could ultimately lead to an elimination of their jobs. The company needed to figure out how to enthusiastically motivate employees to participate in lean, knowing they would understand jobs would be eliminated.

How did Markem management proceed? By creating a team of managers and individual contributors who developed a policy to support lean management while reassuring the workforce the outcome of lean would not cost them their jobs.

This policy was called the "Redeployment Policy," and it began by stating the principles of redeployment. These principles are listed on the next page to give you an idea of the foundation behind the process steps within the policy itself.

Principles of Markem Redeployment Policy

"We will maintain the value of "integrity" in ensuring that we are "open and direct" at the earliest and most appropriate time in communicating with employees whose jobs are affected. This is important both within the community of MARKEM and in the context of the external view of MARKEM as an employer.

We will seek to find internal employment solutions for employees whose jobs are affected by Rapid Improvement Events (Lean events). We will follow a well-defined process that enables employees to be treated fairly and consistently within the company.

When we redeploy human resources, we will endeavor to make the best decisions for both the employee and the business. This means that we will put people in positions where they have the best chance to be successful. Likewise, we will not keep people in positions where they are failing.

We will ensure that legal requirements and practices are carried out wherever we have redeployment issues.

Our redeployment practices will be carried out in such a way as to ensure that we do not decrease or reduce the quality of our products or service to our customers. We will take every reasonable step to ensure that our internal process changes serve to not only maintain our customer service, but in fact, to improve it when possible with applicable process and resource changes.

We will seek to carry out our redeployment of resources in a way that considers and protects the long-term health of the business. As such, the company will maintain the right to utilize management discretion with respect to redeployment decisions or actions as necessary."[19]

The Markem Redeployment Policy provided a step-by-step process where displaced employees were reassigned to other jobs within the company. If, after following this process, there was no job match found for an employee who was displaced, the employee was put on temporary assignment to the Continuous Improvement organization, where the individual worked on lean events.

This policy not only supported the "process and policy" spoke of the performance wheel, but it was an element of the "talent utilization" spoke as well. In fact, the policy spoke volumes about Markem's concern and care for its employees and the company's intention to keep people employed.

For three years following the launch of the Redeployment Policy, there were only a small number of employees who needed to be assigned temporarily to the Continuous Improvement organization, meaning we hadn't found a position for them.

Also, the Redeployment Policy impacted the "recognition and rewards" spoke of the performance wheel. In line with the company's values and culture, redeployed people who were displaced didn't suffer immediate compensation loss regardless of the position they were assigned to. If the compensation range of the new position was lower than the actual compensation of the individual being reassigned, the affected person maintained his/her current compensation for one year. Following this twelve-month period, the compensation was adjusted to the maximum level of the salary range of the new position in accordance with the salary grade at the time of review.

By studying the example of lean management as an HCI, we've seen how multiple spokes of the performance wheel are integrated with the values and culture of the company. For non-process based initiatives, the "process and policy" spoke should be used in conjunction with the other spokes of the performance wheel. When this occurs, they are secondary to the selected HCI, and complementary to other spokes in the performance wheel. An example of process and policy management being in a secondary role would be when supporting an HCI such as "globalization." Processes and policies would be formulated, articulated, and implemented to support globalization actions taking place in areas such as organizational structure, compensation, and hiring practices, to name a few.

Policy Management: An Underappreciated Tool

According to Management Study Guide, an online management tutorial service, "*Business Policy defines the scope or spheres within which decisions can be taken by the subordinates in an organization. It permits the lower level management to deal with the problems and issues without consulting top-level management every time for decisions. Business policies are the guidelines developed by an organization to govern its actions.*" [20]

Policy-based management is described by WhatIs.com in a complementary way to business policy: "*Policy-based management is an administrative approach that is used to simplify the management of a given endeavor by establishing policies to deal with situations that are likely to occur.*" They define policies as "*operating rules that can be referred to as a way to maintain order, security, consistency, or otherwise further a goal or mission.*" [21]

Many organizations don't spend the time on policy management that they should, as it's often thought of as a luxury to write "documentation" for issues needing to be dealt with in real-time. Others believe it's unwise to write policies for fear of setting precedents and thereby establishing legal contracts.

For example, managers may choose to forego written formal policy documents for severances and benefits provided to laid-off employees. They may believe this will allow them the freedom to change the benefits that they provide in the event of a future layoff. This may or may not be true depending upon what the company's past practice is in providing severances and benefits.

The reality though, is that companies take more risks by not writing and communicating their policies, including severance policies. With the proper approach, policies can usually be updated to accommodate business needs.

Human Capital Management includes the proper utilization of policy management. Good written policies help clarify issues for both managers and employees. They can eliminate misunderstandings that can occur, and they can help organizations drive consistency and stability. For those organizations thinking that policies get in the way of situational management, principles can be developed and built into the policies allowing for flexibility according to different situations.

In Human Capital Management, there are a number of policies that should be written and provided to the workforce to bolster the values and culture of the company. Many times these policies are written in general language in documents such as an employee handbook. One problem is that employee handbooks don't provide enough specificity to the workforce regarding the details of the policy and how the process to execute the policy is to be carried out. As a result, when an employee has questions, they need to ask someone for an interpretation of the policy.

It's easy for companies to maintain an active online, real-time version of policies on their intranet. There are plenty of policy subject areas, and it's advisable for companies who aspire to excel in Human Capital Management to ensure the following subject areas are well covered:

- **Legal**: Workplace harassment, equal employment opportunity, etc.

- **Employment and HR related**: Layoffs, standards of conduct, probationary periods, types of employment, compensation, etc.

- **Work environment**: Hours of work, dress codes, workplace hygiene, etc.

- **General Practices**: Emergency closings, external communications, etc.

While it's not my intention to delve deeply into any one of these policy areas, the point is that all of these topics should reflect the desired culture of the organization, and they should support the HCIs.

In the case of Markem's introduction of lean management, the company's decision to modify its policies regarding movement of people within and out of the organization according to the Redeployment Policy helped contribute to the initiative's success.

When I was an executive at Schlumberger, it was very well known inside the company that relatives wouldn't be hired to work within the same company. This was a questionable policy for some of us, considering that during the late 90's competition for good people was fierce. Nonetheless, it was part of the company's culture not to mix relatives in the work environment to avoid conflict-of-interest situations.

This was just the opposite at Markem Corporation where there were a great number of relatives working within the same company. Being a family-held business in a small city, the company's policy regarding family employment was historically based, and practical.

There's no right answer regarding the suitability of close relatives working in the same company, although most experts would agree that relatives shouldn't work within the same management structure. What's more important is that in Schlumberger and Markem, there was a direct correlation between policy management and company culture.

There is one last subject area regarding policies I'd like to cover before moving on. This is the topic of "management." Most companies I worked at didn't have specific manager policy manuals. If they did have them, they were outdated and not operational. A manager policy manual can be of great value. It provides instructions for managers with respect to how a manager should handle certain situations, and it provides process steps to support the policy.

Having observed managers and supervisors at all levels of management throughout my career, I can state with some level of authority that having a manager policy manual is a tremendous advantage. I've seen many occasions where managers in organizations without such policies, unionized or non-unionized, have incorrectly executed what they thought was the correct policy decision, only to have a made a mistake.

There should be a close connection between the "process and policies" spoke in the Human Capital Management System and the other spokes in the system. The processes and policies should be aligned with the tangible programs and activities of all of the spokes.

In particular, there is one specific point to make regarding the relationship between the "organizational structure" spoke and the "processes and policies" spoke. As we've seen in the previous chapter, an organizational structure should be supported by a clear definition of the roles and responsibilities of people within the organization. This is most logically achieved through job descriptions, but they aren't enough. Organizations are living, breathing organisms, where defined roles and responsibilities often overlap between individuals who perform different functions. In order for roles and responsibilities to be carried out as planned, it's important for key processes to be established, and to set policies outlining the rules of the organization.

The combination of these structures, processes, and policies is primarily what should drive the operational behavior of the organization as it seeks to accomplish its mission. Nonetheless, in the majority of instances when I've been an observer of organizational structure changes, the changes in structure were announced to the organization before anyone considered how the decision-making processes and policies would be impacted.

Making changes in an organizational structure before deciding how processes and policies will be impacted causes confusion in an organization. For example, if an organization moves from a "functional" organization structure to a "geographic" organization structure without outlining how decisions impacting pricing discounts are to be made, then there will be a period of time where the different functions within the organization are out of sync.

Many organizations will offset this challenge by advising employees to follow current processes and policies until they're informed otherwise, but what happens when organizational changes eliminate the decision-makers from process decisions they were formerly involved in?

It's clear we can't recreate and rewrite all processes and policies before making organizational structure changes. In fact, many times it's preferred for the newly appointed managers to have a say in determining the processes and policies for which they will be responsible. For processes and policies where organizational functions overlap though, it's more beneficial if the most critical four or five process and policies are updated to account for organizational structure changes that will occur.

Remember, for a workforce to have a strong influence as an organizational weapon, structural changes must be seamless to the organization. Employees spend more time looking for the right answers and deciding whom they should follow when they're confused by management decisions. Sound process and policy management linked to other system elements contributes to good Human Capital Management.

Chapter 12
Talent Utilization:
Right People @ Right Place

Many business leaders point to talent acquisition and talent management as the answer to leveraging organizational talent. This belief is logical as US demographics show there is and will be an ensuing dearth of talent in the decades to come. Numerous experts have predicted demographic trends will create a talent vacuum and there will be fierce competition for scarce human resources.

With the Internet and dot.com boom in the 90's, we've seen the war for talent in most industries, and especially in professional fields fueled by the dot.com era. Compensation packages reached historic highs during this period. Even blue-chip companies with strong brands saw their employees bolting for get-rich stock offerings of start-ups sprouting up all over the country. Dot.com companies promising huge stock options and what appeared to be greener pastures wooed mid-level and senior managers from many of these companies.

In early 2000, as a part of a special assignment in Schlumberger, I was asked to examine and recommend solutions to the recruiting and retention challenges presented by the dot.com craze. Schlumberger was willing to "raise the ante" by giving higher share grants on a more frequent basis to a greater population of contributors, but we weren't willing to offer rich stock-option packages that small start-ups were offering.

I remember reading an article in which GE's CEO, Jack Welsh was asked about the same challenge his organization faced in recruiting and retaining people. Jack was resolute in his convictions that GE wasn't about to battle with start-ups over compensation.

His stance was that GE's value proposition for its employees and managers was something different from what the start-ups were offering. He wasn't embarrassed or apologetic about GE's position, nor was he interested in competing with the start-ups. As a prospective employer, Jack suggested GE was different. He didn't say GE was unwilling to offer competitive compensation packages. He did say GE was not a quick hit company. Managers and executives would need to prove themselves over a prolonged period of time to reach the senior ranks and enjoy the compensation packages these positions merited.

The same was true at Schlumberger. Simply relying on compensation as the solution was shortsighted. Instead, we sought prospective employees who were looking for company characteristics that fit with what we were offering. While our compensation model was adjusted to offer small stock option grants to a larger number of managers, our primary efforts were in two different areas: ensuring we were attracting the right candidates, and ensuring our best and brightest were continuously engaged and challenged.

As a result of the dot.com era, "talent management" became the prevailing new buzzwords. SuccessFactors, an SAP company specializing in business and performance execution software refers to talent management as follows:

"Talent management refers to the process of attracting, selecting, training, developing and promoting employees through an organization." [22]

I like this definition because it's specific about elements of the system included in talent management. One should note though, that the components included in this definition cross the sub-functional HR areas of "recruiting," "organizational development," and indirectly areas such as "compensation." One could argue that talent management touches any area related to people management.

The Society of Human Resource Management (SHRM) refers to talent management as *"...the implementation of integrated strategies or systems designed to increase workplace productivity by developing improved processes for attracting, developing, retaining, and utilizing people with the required skills and aptitude to meet current and future business needs."* [23]

The SHRM definition is meaningful as it suggests the elements of the system need to be integrated to be effective.

In my opinion, talent management comes up short as a practice. It's difficult to manage as a single entity because it includes a wide array of HR sub-functions. For example, at the operational level, managers who have skills in recruitment may not have the skills to manage training and employee development. Proponents of talent management include several sub-functions of the HR discipline when referring to comprehensive talent management. Advocates sometimes include compensation as a component of talent management since it plays a role in the attraction, recruitment, and retention of individuals. As a result, the practice of talent management has become blurred because the definition has been watered down.

There are other aspects of Human Capital Management beyond talent management that have an impact on the attraction, recruitment, and retention of people. For example, a company's organizational structure affects reporting relationships and the levels of interaction employees have with management. Similarly, a company's communication program may not be included in talent management, but could be a factor in employee retention.

To summarize, talent management represents a combination of HR sub-functions, but in my opinion, it shouldn't be organized as a practice by itself, as it contains too many sub-functions to be effectively managed.

"Talent acquisition" is another popular term. Talent acquisition is much more than just recruiting and staffing and is viewed as a business process or in the parlance of lean management, a value stream. According to Matt Rivera, writing on the site of The Seamless Workforce:

"Talent acquisition is the ongoing cycle of processes related to attracting, sourcing, recruiting, and hiring (or placing) employees within an organization. This includes elements of employment branding, outreach, networking, and relationship building with potential candidate communities to continually build and enhance the talent pool for an organization." [24]

Talent acquisition is narrower than talent management, but it's beyond what one sub-function should have responsibility to manage. To make this point, let's look at the creation of an "employment brand." For those unfamiliar with an employment brand, it refers to the reputation or perception that perspective candidates and employees have of the company. The employment brand is what differentiates or distinguishes a company, and what makes it special as an employer. Many companies proactively develop an employment brand and work to reinforce it so that it's consistent and aligned with their desired image.

Some proponents of talent acquisition believe those managing the talent acquisition sub-functions should manage employment branding. Yet, employment branding isn't a concept beneficial only for the purpose of talent acquisition. It's also a link to the company's culture and internal branding for retention purposes. As such, employment branding needs to support all the components of the performance wheel, regardless of who owns the branding responsibility itself.

Similar to talent management, talent acquisition is needed for an effective Human Capital Management System. There's no disputing talent acquisition as a critical component to the success of an organization, but there's more to success in building a capable workforce than simply hiring the best and the brightest.

Throughout the history of sports, there are plenty of teams that had the best players, but didn't win championships. Nor can everyone on a team be the star player. There have to be individuals who play specific roles for the team to achieve its goals.

Certainly, in order to perform well, every sports team or business entity needs to have some top performers. In sports, just as in business, at every level, there are "good," "better," and "best" players. All three of these categories of people are needed to play their roles effectively if the organization is to win.

In any business, there are only so many of the "best and brightest." The availability of talent is in the shape of a bell curve. In any organization or workforce availability pool, there's only a small percentage of top talent just as there's a small percentage of bottom talent. Most of the talent pool is made up of average or above average people. These are the "good" and "better" people, but not the "best."

The reality for most employers is that attracting and keeping top talent isn't feasible on a consistent, repetitive, and long-term basis. There are only so many GEs, IBMs, and Googles who have the brand power to attract and hire the best and the brightest. The blue-chip, well known companies who consistently perform at a high level will maintain themselves as the preferred companies to work for, and as long as they can keep their position as leaders in their chosen markets, they will have an edge in attracting top talent.

So what about the rest of the companies who need talented people?

The name of the game for most organizations is to have the "right" talent, not necessarily the "best" talent. These organizations need a small percentage of top players who will be counted on to lead the company in key positions, but in any organization, if only 20% of the people are contributing to overall performance, the remaining 80% are either a financial drain or an opportunity cost. In companies who strive to practice Human Capital Management, the idea is to involve not only the top 20%, but also the majority of people that make up the "good" and "better" people to gain an advantage.

The former CEO of Dover Product Identification, Omar Kerbage, regularly spoke about what he called ensuring we had "RP@RP" or "the right people in the right place or position." This became part of our human capital strategy as we sought to achieve our business strategy.

One of the principles that companies like GE and Schlumberger knew and practiced during the late 90's and still do today, is the importance of finding people who are the right fit for them. They want to attract and hire those interested in what the company has to offer over the long-term.

Whether leading a blue-chip company or a smaller organization without a strong brand name, organizational leaders are appropriately concerned about finding the best talent and keeping them. Talent is scarce. Talent acquisition and talent management are key areas for organizations to concentrate on when seeking to leverage their workforce as a competitive advantage. But they're only part of the equation.

In Human Capital Management, **"talent utilization" more aptly describes what we're attempting to achieve in attracting, sourcing, selecting, hiring, placing, and utilizing the individual and collective talents of our workforce. Talent utilization includes talent acquisition, but it stops short of talent management since sub-functional areas such as "organizational development" and "recognition, rewards, and remuneration" are separate spokes in the performance wheel.** In the Human Capital Management System, these spokes carry a heavy weight and value, and as such, represent individual spokes, even though they're closely related to one another.

What distinguishes talent utilization from both talent acquisition and talent management is the action of "placing" and "utilizing" individuals and teams appropriately to ensure the right people are in the right place. In Human Capital Management, the placement and utilization of people is just as critical as talent acquisition.

The remainder of this chapter will cover three particular sub-topics of talent utilization to emphasize their importance within the Human Capital Management System. These sub-topics include attracting the right candidates, building an employment brand, and managing the RP@RP employment life cycle.

Additionally, a few examples will be provided regarding talent utilization ideas that can work for any organization looking to improve its capabilities to attract, hire, and keep people from going elsewhere.

Attract the "Right" Candidates, not the "Best" Candidates

Many recruiters attempt to attract a high volume of candidates to fill their job openings, thinking "more is better." The smart recruiters know good recruiting comes from finding the "right" candidates. These are the candidates most likely to fit in with the company, having had a good track record as employees, and being more likely to stay with the company beyond the first couple of years.

When it comes to motivating the workforce as a whole, it's disruptive to have high turnover and employees who are disgruntled or unhappy. When the workforce has a positive and like mindset, it's easier to motivate and inspire them to do great things.

I have three recommendations for organizations regarding how they should approach attracting the right candidates. The first recommendation is to **market and sell the company the same as you would any product you're trying to sell.** A lot of companies would say they already take this approach. When I hear people say this, I ask them who in their organization determines when, where, and how they will recruit for openings. The answer is usually "the HR Department with input from the hiring manager."

Companies serious about marketing and selling themselves to attract the right candidates should make the most of their Marketing organization. The Marketing function should help formulate a recruiting strategy based on the 4 P's of marketing: Product, Position or Place (placement of the product), Promotion, and Price. Price is perhaps the only one of the 4 P's where HR should take the lead.

The marketing and selling of the company and/or job should include a formalized process where the product's features and benefits are articulated in writing, and based on identifying the best markets to target and sell to. Then a sourcing strategy and tactical action plan should be created.

The marketing approach to recruiting should reflect the values and culture of the company, and make use of the company's strengths in determining the tactical actions to attract the right people.

Over twenty years ago, I was a mid-level HR manager in Silicon Valley, working at Schlumberger's Automated Test Equipment division. The core business of the company was designing, manufacturing, and selling automated test equipment for the semiconductor industry. At the time, the company was organized by product line, and one of the main product families was the Diagnostic Systems division.

The President of the Diagnostic Systems division was a brilliant engineer in his early 30's named Neil Richardson, who is still an active business leader in Silicon Valley today. Well regarded as the godfather of the focused electron beam tester, Neil was masterful as a recruiter as he was consistently able to attract top notch, quality candidates, and rarely did they leave the company after joining.

There were a number of factors contributing to Neil's capability to recruit his team. First, every one of his employees was constantly scanning the industry for potential candidates who had the technical capabilities, intelligence, and quest for excellence that were common characteristics within the Diagnostic Systems team. Additionally, Neil and members of his team sometimes gave technical presentations at places like Stanford University and the California Institute of Technology where they generated substantial interest from potential candidates. In fact, Neil was so successful generating enthusiasm for would-be employees on occasion his own customers would approach him or someone on his team to ask about the possibility of joining them.

Neil walked into my office multiple times and casually remarked that he or someone in his team had found a worthy individual that we should bring in for an interview. During the four years I worked with Neil, we hired numerous people for his growing business unit. What was most remarkable about his recruiting approach is that the company didn't spend one dollar on any form of mass recruiting, job advertisements or recruiting agencies.

Once a job offer was made to a candidate, it was rare for the individual to lose the hook. Candidates would typically spend a whole day with employees from the Diagnostic Systems group. Neil insisted managerial candidates had to be interviewed by their prospective subordinates before this became a popular practice. Despite my reservations at the time, this practice worked just fine, and helped contribute to the assimilation of new hires. It was motivational to employees who participated in the recruiting process as well. No matter the level of reporting relationship, Neil made it a practice to call the candidate personally after a job offer was made. It was great modeling of the personalized approach and commitment that was part of the marketing strategy being applied for recruitment, and a great way to close a sale. New hires who were one or two levels removed from the reporting relationship to Neil were flattered that he would call them, and they often remarked that this phone call made a positive difference in their decision to join the company.

The Diagnostic Systems management team took their ownership role in recruitment very seriously. Neil and his team were masterful in taking a marketing approach to the talent acquisition process. It was the one time in my career where HR was a very minimal player in the recruiting process, and frankly I never saw it work better.

As one might expect, Neil continued to have a successful career, leaving Schlumberger to become Executive Vice President in charge of metrology products at KLA-Tencor, and more recently served as CEO of Gemfire Corporation. He continues to be a venture capital partner in Silicon Valley today.

My second recommendation is to **ensure the inside view of your organization's identity and reputation is consistent with the external marketplace (vendors, customers, etc.) view.** This requires taking tangible actions to find out how your organization is perceived externally. This step should be taken in the early stages in the formulation of the marketing strategy to attract the right candidates. It's also a key to crafting an employment brand.

There are a number of ways to achieve an external scan by combining with other marketing projects such as customer and vendor surveys, voice of the customer focus groups, customer advisory boards, and the like. Additionally, prospective employees and exiting employees are excellent sources of feedback when obtaining information to help evaluate whether the internal view of an organization is accurate. In the world of selling products of any kind, the customer's perception is reality.

Let me share another experience I had while working in Silicon Valley. This time, the example comes from the Component

Test division, a sister company of the Diagnostic Systems division mentioned earlier.

In contrast to the Diagnostic Systems division, the Component Test division had greater challenges in recruiting and retaining people. At the time, the Component Test division didn't have a strong product position in the marketplace, and the division was losing money. Employee turnover was higher than desired, and recruiting was limited to critical replacements only.

As part of the company's recruiting program, the Component Test division participated in the renowned MIT-6A program, which matched up electrical engineering students from the Massachusetts Institute of Technology with internship positions in technology-based companies. The program was expensive and the company spent approximately $6,000 per student, plus a housing allowance to boot.

The Component Test division participated in the MIT-6A internship program each of the four years I was affiliated with the division. During this period, we averaged 3-4 interns per summer, and over the four years, we probably invested close to $100,000 in the MIT-6A program. Students appreciated the work experience with us and well-respected technologists mentored them. They also loved living on the west coast for the summer months where they had the luxury of consistently sunny and warm weather, and the lifestyles that accompany it.

Despite making job offers to former interns who sometimes worked two or three summers with us, the Component Test division convinced only one MIT-6A student to join the company as a full-time employee during this period. After conducting interviews with the students who rejected these job offers, their reasons for declining these jobs were most often attributed to the fact that they didn't find the technology as interesting. In addition, the profitability of the company was a concern, and the reputation of the company wasn't at its best in the industry.

Despite this lack of success, the Component Test division continued to pour money into a losing proposition because those of us in management positions weren't honest enough with ourselves about who we were as a company. We incorrectly assessed the strength of our brand, and we were drawn in by the glamor of recruiting MIT students.

Perhaps the decision to continue unsuccessfully with the MIT-6A internships was influenced by our mistaken belief regarding our attractiveness as a Silicon Valley company. I remember having a conversation with a high-level executive who was visiting from our European-based corporate headquarters. He couldn't understand why our efforts to recruit MIT graduates were unsuccessful and he suggested we analyze what we were doing wrong and encouraged us to continue with the program. In Europe, where the company's headquarters were, it was one of the most well-known and respected companies in any industry. But in the USA, the company was lesser known.

Knowing who you are and who you aren't is essential to ensuring your marketing and selling strategy for attracting candidates is credible. If not, sometimes we learn the hard way by wasting time or money, which ultimately impacts business results.

The third recommendation regarding attracting the right candidates is to **make sure the marketing approach aligns with the core values and culture of the company. In other words, market who you are. If the values and the culture are an accurate reflection of your organization's personality, then you want to target your efforts at recruiting those who will fit within this culture.**

Many companies now develop interview techniques and questions to test for cultural fit, but simply put, company culture needs to be dealt with in the recruiting process at the sourcing stage, not only at the interview stage. Organizations that pursue sources of talent based on values and cultural fit will have a higher percentage of recruiting success.

Let me share an example that supports this point. As indicated earlier, Markem's corporate headquarters were in Keene, New Hampshire. Keene is a small city of less than 30,000 people and is located in the southwest corner of the state. As a product identification company, the company designed, manufactured, and sold coding and marking machines and supplies including inks. This required several different types of engineering talent such as electrical engineers, software engineers, and chemical engineers. Keene is a quaint community, and it has a special New England charm. The old-school look of its downtown area makes one feel like the clock has been turned back in time. But regardless of its small town appeal, attracting and recruiting people to Keene was a challenge.

Boston was located only two hours away, but despite attempts to find people there, our efforts to attract big-city people to Keene were unsuccessful. Our recruiting attention turned to a cross-section of much smaller cities, and companies sharing values similar to our own. One of these cities was Rochester, NY where there were companies in markets similar or adjacent to marking and coding. Another was Worchester, Massachusetts, with a population of less than 200,000 and named five times as an All-American City. Located less than 100 miles away, it was the home of Worchester Polytechnic Institute, an excellent recruiting source for us to target given its Engineering & Computer Science and Chemical Engineering programs.

Concentrating our recruiting efforts in areas more demographically similar to our own generated a candidate pool more likely to fit with our company culture, and ultimately improved our "time to hire" and "cost per hire." Casting a wide net and hoping the right fish will jump in isn't the best way to fish. Its better to find the kind of streams your fish swim in, and catch the ones you're looking for.

Enlisting the Marketing function to develop a strategy for attracting the right candidates, ensuring the internal and external identity of the organization is consistent, and aligning these with the core values and culture of the company is a powerful combination. Aside from sharpening the organization's ability to find the right candidates, this effort will also save time and money.

Using the Employment Brand as a Lever

The employment brand is a misunderstood concept. In the view of many, especially those in talent acquisition, it's about defining an image so prospective employees will view the organization as a great place to work. **The employment brand should be used to strive for a better cultural fit in attracting the right job candidates, but also to increase the level of engagement, motivation, and retention in the current workforce of an organization.**

We would all like our companies to be known as a great place to work, but producing an employment brand is more about communicating the organization's identity through its brand. Its purpose is to provide a view of this identity, for attracting the right candidates and for maintaining a consistent internal image of what the organization should be for its employees. It's another management tool that should reflect the values, culture, and personality of the organization.

The employment brand must be linked to the corporate brand and to the product brand. While each of these brands may be directed at separate audiences, consistency is necessary to maintain integrity and credibility of the messaging for all three. This seems logical, but plenty of organizations don't connect their corporate brand to their product brand or to their employment brand, and there is a simple reason why.

Different functions and people are typically responsible for developing the corporate, product, and employment brands. For those large-scale organizations with corporate communications functions, they often work top-down in creating branding messages. In other words, the messaging is fashioned at the corporate level sometimes without regard to what's happening at the product line levels below. It's not uncommon for corporate communications people to inform their subsidiary organizations or product groups to follow the corporate brand. This may be the case because they feel a bottom-up approach to branding may be too challenging given the number of different constituencies they have to blend into the messaging. Another simple explanation is corporate communications departments don't want their subsidiary brands to influence the top-level branding. They may feel that inviting subsidiary input into corporate branding brings "too many cooks into the kitchen."

Product branding is typically owned by Marketing, and employment branding is typically managed by Human Resources. However, the best approach is for Marketing and HR to partner together when creating the employment brand. If there's a Marketing Communications or Corporate Communications function separate from Marketing, these functions should all work together with HR to create the employment brand. It's the best way to ensure compatibility of all branding activities.

Depending on what survey you read, no more than half the companies in the USA have formalized their employment branding programs. This means there are plenty of organizations that have an opportunity to improve their ability to attract the right people and build a stronger identity for their current workforce. For those who need help building an employment brand, there are an abundance of consulting and marketing companies available to offer assistance. To get started, I recommend using a free online tool offered by Career Builder, called "Start Branding." It's a good presentation on the topic of Employment Branding. You can find this in the link below:

http://www.careerbuildercommunications.com/pdf/employmentbrandebook.pdf

Understanding the "RP@RP Employment Life Cycle"

Having the "right people at the right place" is what separates talent utilization from both talent acquisition and talent management. Talent acquisition is about getting talent into the organization. Talent management is focused primarily on the combination of talent acquisition and organizational development, but with other components like compensation as well.

Talent utilization includes talent acquisition, but goes further to ensure the right people are in the right place on a continuous basis to maximize their effectiveness as individual contributors and as members of a highly functioning workforce.

As pointed out earlier, organizational development is critical, but treated as a separate component in the performance wheel. In the "RP@RP Employment Life Cycle" the main efforts are on the role of the individual and as a member of a team or organization.

In this regard, let's look at performance and potential relative to value and impact on organizational performance. The matrix in Figure 14 below shows a range of suitable employer actions relative to the employee's performance and potential. In each quadrant, the basic description shows the result of the performance/potential combination, and then below it, the appropriate action to be taken regarding the employee's employment status. In each case, training may be appropriate to improve performance as well.

Figure 14

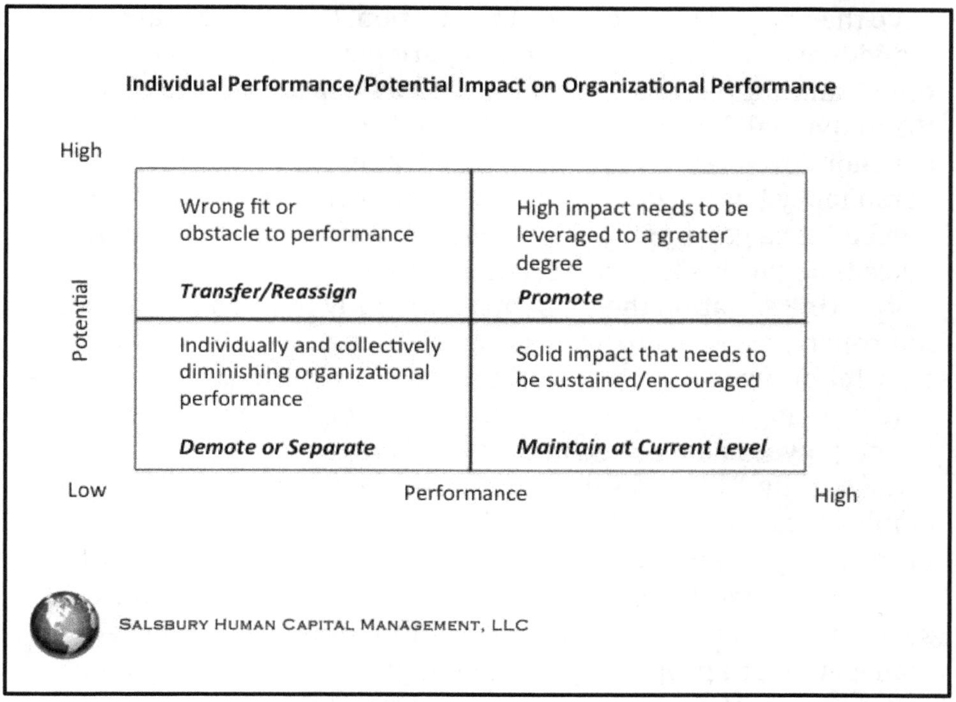

	Individual Performance/Potential Impact on Organizational Performance	
High	Wrong fit or obstacle to performance	High impact needs to be leveraged to a greater degree
	Transfer/Reassign	*Promote*
Potential	Individually and collectively diminishing organizational performance	Solid impact that needs to be sustained/encouraged
	Demote or Separate	*Maintain at Current Level*
Low	Performance	**High**

SALSBURY HUMAN CAPITAL MANAGEMENT, LLC

As the bottom-left quadrant shows, when there is a period of poor performance deemed unacceptable, action needs to take place to either separate the employee from employment or move the person to a job he/she can do more effectively. Poor performance combined with poor potential is a drain on the organization, and if there are too many of these situations, there's a negative draw on the time and energy of management, ultimately decreasing the overall effectiveness of the workforce.

In the upper-left quadrant, the employee has good potential but poor performance. This can occur for any number of reasons but in my opinion the most common reason is that the person doesn't have the appropriate skills for the position. It could be that the individual is new in the job. After a period of induction and time/training, performance will probably improve. It could be that the individual doesn't have the required skills for the position, and may not develop the skills, even with training. In other cases, the person may have been transferred, promoted cross-functionally or moved into a geographic region outside their home country, and it takes time for this kind of adjustment to produce results.

One situation that happens frequently is when employees are improperly assigned to a position, either as a new hire or through a transfer or promotion. Management sometimes makes the mistake of identifying this as a performance problem and in many instances the employee is dismissed because he/she can't perform the job satisfactorily. This is disappointing and unproductive for both the employee and the organization since the individual may have been performing well in the former position. It highlights the importance of verifying that the individual has the requisite skills before selection is made. It also underscores the commitment needed from management to properly guide and nurture an individual when that person is transferred or promoted to a "stretch" job, one that may be outside the core function, industry or geography of the individual.

The quadrant on the bottom-right shows those employees who perform well, but are unlikely to be promoted much higher than their current position. These employees are assets to the company and make up a good portion of the workforce. In particular, some of these employees are "key employees," those who have a particular skill set that is extremely difficult to replicate. A key employee is someone difficult to replace even after a replacement has been hired and has been doing the job for a prolonged period of time. For example, a good CFO is not necessarily a key employee unless he or she has specific skills that are unique to the CFO function.

The position may be an important position, but there are others who can do the job effectively. A key employee is a person with very specialized knowledge and skills very few other people have. It's vital that this group of individuals within the lower-right quadrant is motivated and morale is good for their well-being, but also for them to be positioned effectively as valuable resources in the organization.

The employees in the upper-right quadrant of Figure 14 are strong performers and have good potential to grow within the organization. These people need to be challenged and developed to maximize their own potential, but also to the benefit of the organization. They can be champions for organizational projects and HCIs.

Utilization of this performance/potential matrix, whether it be in this 2x2 box approach or a more sophisticated approach is essential to an organization. First, it can serve as a tracking tool to examine the big picture view of the performance and potential of the total workforce. Second, upon further analysis, it can provide valuable information regarding groups or individuals within the quadrants. Third, it can serve as a benefit in the early planning stages of an HCI, as management decides which individuals should be enlisted as organizational champions or team members for a particular initiative.

"RP@RP" is an indispensable element of high performing human capital management teams. Putting people in the right place to contribute to an organization not only applies to the specific job the employee is assigned to, but also can apply to organizational teams assembled on a continuous basis. The following are examples of organizational roles employees can play, sometimes in addition to their daily individual jobs:

- Serving on a task force

- A temporary assignment

- Serving on a committee

- Serving on a project team

Many times, organizational initiatives are critical to the current and future performance of the business. Every organization needs to have good people performing in their own jobs and in organizational roles too. The challenge for many organizations is when there aren't enough good people to assign to organizational initiatives. The result is the "20%-80% rule," when 20% of the employee population is assigned to 80% of the organizational initiatives. This becomes problematic since organizations tap the same resources over and over again, and management then complains that there aren't enough good people to select for these organizational roles. This is a self-fulfilling prophecy.

Companies need to spend more time and effort cultivating pools of people from the appropriate quadrants of performance/potential, being sure to match up the right people for the right organizational assignments. For example, it makes perfect sense for a high performer/high potential to be enlisted as a champion or leader in launching an HCI. This wouldn't be such a great idea for a person who isn't performing well in his/her current job, regardless of his/her potential.

With serious organizational planning the "20%-80%" problem can be reversed. Getting to a situation where 80% of the employee population is actively participating in organizational initiatives may not be realistic in the near-term, but a strategic approach to building organizational participation can result in at least 50% employee participation without too much difficulty.

There are plenty of ways to build workforce participation, increase employee engagement, and talent utilization. Here are a few simple examples:

- Assemble organizational task forces for initiatives crossing functional boundaries, and select leaders based on performance, skill or potential. Make it a rule that no one can serve as a task force leader more than once in a two-year time frame.

- Make it clear in performance management that employee performance is based on individual job performance and organizational participation.

- Give employees the opportunity to present to upper level management on the results and accomplishments of team initiatives. This not only reinforces organizational participation and motivation of the workforce, but it builds management confidence in trusting people within the organization to accomplish results without being micro-managed.

In Human Capital Management, it's imperative to have the right people in the right job. This can be achieved if:

- The organization does the legwork upfront to appropriately attract the right candidates.

- Employment branding is carried out effectively for internal as well as external candidates.

- Selection of the right people for the right job is carefully made for individual positions and organizational initiatives.

- Management monitors the performance/potential and contribution of employees.

- Management builds an increasing base of talent to draw from to play organizational roles, in addition to specific job roles.

Talent Utilization as a Human Capital Initiative

In the early 90's, there were a tremendous number of companies who caught the fire to go to Asia, and specifically China, as it continued to open up to the West. Schlumberger was no exception, and a management team was established in Asia to manage all of Schlumberger's non-oilfield businesses there. Previous to this organizational setup, all of the employees of each division reported through management levels back to the headquarters of the division. This meant that the Asia employees of Schlumberger Automated Test Equipment reported back to management headquartered in San Jose, CA. Asia employees of Electricity Metering reported to management headquartered in Paris, France, and the same was true for the other businesses.

With the introduction of a new management team in Asia, the former reporting structure became obsolete. All non-oilfield based employees reported to the Asia management team, and the Asia management team reported to Schlumberger's corporate management. I was assigned to the role as Director of HR for the Asia management team.

During this time, the number one mission for the new Asia management team was to grow profitable sales throughout the Asia-Pacific region. In order to make this happen, we needed to hire talented people, including experienced executives who had the expertise to grow and manage businesses, as well as young and dynamic people who had the energy to move in a fast-paced environment. The strategy to grow was multi-faceted, with start-ups in some areas, joint venture activities, and infusion of funds to support organic growth.

One of the most important initiatives was "growing Asia talent within the organization." Not only was there a lack of talented Asians at the entry-level, but the mid-level and executive management ranks were thin as well.

The Asia talent initiative was two-fold. First, we had active operational responsibilities to attract and hire people for the ongoing projects being pursued to grow our revenue base. Second, we knew that as we grew in size, our requirement for talented people at all levels would only be met if we developed a talent pool for future growth. The challenge we had was to invest in people for the future, and still make money in the present.

We went about the business of designing a number of programs to hire and train people from various Asia countries according to our strategic business plan. It was also necessary for us to build new training programs, compensation structures, and other key components. We needed to ensure the policies and processes that we established to drive our internal operations were in line with the fast-paced, high performance culture we were looking to install, while being careful to align them with the core values and corporate culture of Schlumberger.

As I look back on that particular assignment in my career, I can recall some of the mistakes we made in implementing the new organization and more specifically, the Asia talent initiative. Nonetheless, during that period the Asia team had some impressive successes. Buoyed by an influx of talent and resources, the Asia-Pacific region grew in revenue over 90% year over year for three years in a row, starting at $50M. We probably hired over 100 professionals during those years, and the foundation that was laid enabled the company to continue its rapid growth and increased profitability throughout the decade.

This success was a combination of management and employee-led activities enabling the workforce to flourish, and there's no question that without this commitment and motivation of employees, we would never have succeeded. Fortunately there was alignment of the business foundation (mission, vision, values, and culture) with our strategy, and the programs that were put in place. The actions to bring about the Asia talent initiative were integrated with each of the spokes in the performance wheel.

There are a number of talent utilization activities that can serve as an HCI. This can include anything from starting a Greenfield operation to carrying out a merger, and many more. Most of the time these initiatives are linked to growth or productivity, and the best organizations are skillful enough to turn what can sometimes become negative influences into positive successes. This is only possible when the right people have been hired and are in the right assignments.

Chapter 13
Building an Organizational Development Framework

There are numerous definitions of "organizational development" and they are fairly diverse. Some experts even distinguish "organizational development" from Organizational Development, noting the latter is a field of applied behavioral science. I prefer the more simple-to-understand definition, as provided by Jac Fitz-Enz and Barbara Davison, authors of *"How to Measure Human Resources Management."* In visiting the topic of organizational development, they describe it as *"...a planned intervention aimed at improving individual and organizational health and effectiveness."* [25]

In its Glossary of Human Resources Terms, The Society of Human Resource Management (SHRM) defines organizational development as *"a planned organization-wide effort to improve and increase the organization's effectiveness, productivity, return on investment and overall employee job satisfaction through planned interventions in the organization's processes."* [26]

I like this definition because it makes the point that organizational efforts are aimed at the organization's improvement and the employee's job satisfaction that comes through personal development. The definition is somewhat narrow though in characterizing organizational development as an "organization-wide effort." There are many organizational development activities aimed at segments of the workforce that aren't necessarily organization-wide. In addition, interventions often include training and development activities, not just processes.

Understanding How to Deploy The "Hierarchy of Development Needs"

From a practical point of view, the organization's leadership is responsible for the development of programs and processes seeking to achieve productivity improvements and return on investment. Most of the time, senior management, HR, and direct managers lead these activities.

For an individual, there are essentially three ways to develop and grow. These are shown in the Hierarchy of Development Needs in Figure 15 below.

Figure 15

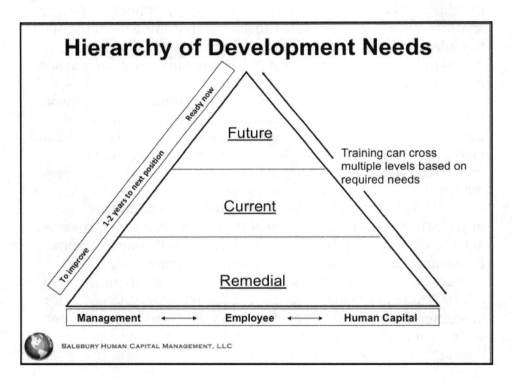

As shown in the pyramid, **the bottom level of employee growth is "remedial," which is essentially a corrective measure(s) to retrain or re-educate an individual so he/she performs successfully in the current position**. The objective of the training is for the employee's performance to improve. Some experts might challenge whether or not remedial is developmental, but in a practical way, development occurs when a person conquers a skill not formerly mastered.

The second level of the pyramid is development in one's current position. This includes activities and training to help the individual perform more successfully and at a higher skill level in the current job.

The individual is ready to move to the third level of the pyramid (labeled as "future" development activities) only when the essential skills of the current position and performance in this position have been mastered. These are activities to assist the individual in adding new skills for jobs beyond the current one.

Training and development activities don't have to be fixed to one level or another. They aren't mutually exclusive. An individual can be developing nicely in his/her current position, and still need remedial training and development in specific areas. The same is true in regards to participation in "current" and "future" training and development activities. The individual him or herself has the foremost responsibility for training and development. It's the direct manager's responsibility to guide a subordinate's development, and typically HR has a role in supporting development as well. While the employee is the main party responsible to seek growth and development, it's management's responsibility to support the actions to achieve growth and ensure that they're relevant, responsible, and credible.

It's a waste of time and money to provide employees with the opportunity to have training they won't be able to use in the near-term. My rule of thumb is if an employee won't benefit from training within an 18-month window or less, it's a waste of effort. One course I have seen attended by the wrong people over and over again is "Finance for the Non-Financial Manager." Some would say this course is worthwhile because it provides generalized management training to "round out" the individual. In my opinion, if the skills will not be applied practically, it's a waste. Why not spend time and money on more appropriate training and development activities that will be beneficial in the near-term. For a young manager, project management or supervisory/management courses are much more relevant.

Organizational development is really no different than individual development. This Hierarchy of Development Needs can work just as well for the organization as it can for the individual. If you think about it, organizations go through the same developmental stages as individuals. Some may be performing well in their current state, but still need some aspects of remedial attention. Similarly, organizations aspiring to a future state need to work on aspects that will help them get there.

When developing new organizational development programs or activities, I've often seen organizations take the "silver bullet" approach. It's the one shot solution aimed at solving the problems or development needs of the company. I've seen multiple organizations embrace "succession planning" as the single solution to its overall management and leadership challenges, and realize three years later they were in no better position to name position replacements than when they started.

The solution to this problem is to think about organizational development as an overall framework. The Free Dictionary defines the word "framework" as *"a structure for supporting or enclosing something else, especially a skeletal support used as the basis for something being constructed."*[27]

The framework is only a skeleton or backbone for programs and activities linking directly to the development needs of the organization. More specifically, the organizational development framework should support the HCIs coming from the business strategy and organizational goals.

Take a look at the Organizational Development Framework in Figure 16 below.

Figure 16

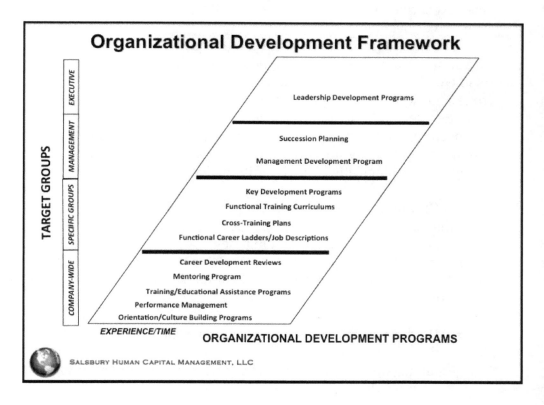

This chart shows groups identified in an organization as "targets" to be considered for training and development needs. The first group is the organization as a whole, shown in the chart identified as "company-wide." This includes all the employees. Programs in this category include company culture building programs, and other activities or programs all employees should have access to.

The next category is what I call "specific groups," and could include programs based on groups of employees from a specific part of the organization according to geography, function, high potential or key employee groups.

The third and fourth groups are "management" and "leadership" respectively. At the management level, there may be a development program within the company tailored to basic management skills. At the leadership level, identified in the chart as the "executive" level, there may be specific programs such as executive coaching.

I should point out that the programs listed in the framework are simply examples and aren't meant to be an exhaustive list. It's also worth noting the chart slants from left to right to indicate more time and experience required as programs move up the chart. One would expect an individual contributor fresh out of college to be exposed to a company's cultural training programs immediately upon employment, whereas executive or leadership training programs will logically come later in one's career.

Organizational development programs should be complementary to one another. Executives and HR leaders who have the responsibility for organizational development should build an organizational development framework for their company before initiating individual programs, and in doing so, answer the following questions:

- Do the activities or programs in the organizational development framework support the selected human capital management initiatives? If they can't be directly correlated, why are they on the list?

- Do the activities or programs in the organizational development framework fit with the non-human capital organizational goals? For example, if the organization has committed to developing an HSE (health, safety, and environment) training program owned by a function outside of HR, is it within the organizational development framework?

- After listing and vetting these activities and programs, have they been prioritized and planned for in a comprehensive manner? What are the selected programs for the next 12 months vs. those to be worked on in the second year, and then the third year?

Using Organizational Development as a Human Capital Initiative

Let me share an experience I had as an executive at Dover. Beginning around the year 2008, Dover Corporation was in the process of transitioning from a very decentralized conglomerate of approximately 50 companies to a more homogenized corporation. The decentralization of the past had been a hallmark of Dover's success in keeping their companies independent and thus allowed them to maintain close relationships with their customers and markets, unencumbered by corporate bureaucracy. But times had changed as Dover sought to improve its profit margins and efficiencies for the purpose of improving its price-earnings ratio.

In general, integrated companies have a better built-in advantage to creating efficiencies than decentralized companies. Knowing this, Dover began a process of transition to a new and improved corporation seeking to improve the bottom line by leveraging support functions such as Supply Chain Management and other staff functions. Part of the formula was to allow the subsidiary companies to keep ownership of their commercial related functions.

Profitability isn't the only impact decentralization had on Dover's operations. One of the other consequences was Dover's limited formalization of succession planning at all but the top of the organization. In many of its subsidiaries, if subordinate Vice Presidents were not immediately prepared to replace the President, the company often went outside to find a replacement, most typically looking for someone with industry experience. Promotions to key positions appeared to be managed more at the subsidiary level than at the corporate level. Dover senior management decided to strengthen and develop its senior leadership, and make it a cornerstone of its new business strategy.

There were other components of the business strategy as well, but the human capital leadership initiative was critical to Dover's ability to meet its long-term strategic goals.

As a kick-off to this initiative, a task force was organized, bringing together a number of subsidiary presidents and HR leaders from throughout the corporation. The initial meeting of the task force was held in Chicago and the team began to build a set of leadership competencies for use in conjunction with the establishment of a corporate-wide succession planning program.

As the Dover executives debated the various leadership competencies and behaviors to be included in the program, it became abundantly clear to the team that this project was larger than the sole objective of simply identifying leadership competencies.

The task force members understood leadership competencies needed to reflect the personality and strategy of the organization, its culture and values. Interestingly, Dover had a rich cultural tradition and unwritten values, but management had not previously spread these values across the corporation due to its decentralized approach. Many of the subsidiary companies had their own values.

As the project got underway, the objective of the task force was enlarged to include the development of core values as well as leadership competencies. But that wasn't all. The task force and Dover leadership team also realized there were a number of other interrelated programs needing attention.

As a result, a number of sub-initiatives were developed in phase I of the overall leadership initiative, and they're briefly summarized below:

- The "Dover Values and Leadership Competencies" were introduced together through a series of communications including brochures and other written materials, as well as a video production of Dover's CEO presenting the values. These were then communicated across the organization consistently and repeatedly with the aid of a marketing communications package to position them effectively. Naturally, the foundation for the leadership competencies was based on the core values as a starting point.

- Dover's senior management understood that in order for these leadership competencies to be effective in driving the behavior of executives and managers within the corporation, they needed to be strengthened by evaluating management against the competencies. As such, an evaluation system was constructed for review of executives and managers from top management at the corporate and subsidiary levels.

- The company needed to develop processes and tools for its succession planning program. This was a major undertaking with a variety of decisions to be made for the program to be executed efficiently and professionally.

- Finally, the company needed to integrate each of these programs and tools. This included determination of appropriate technology to serve as an online tool to help manage the evaluation of leadership competencies within a formalized succession planning system. SuccessFactors was chosen as the vendor to provide this deliverable for Dover.

In total, it took approximately two years for Dover to put all of these interrelated programs and tools into action and make them fully functional. To the credit of those who led the effort, they solicited the active participation of several different executives across the corporation to participate in working groups along the way. This is a real example of a company that blended a cross-section of its management team to build enthusiasm and shape an important HCI.

The initiative was integrated with other spokes of the performance wheel. For example, the company's corporate executive compensation structure was reestablished as a sister project. The new executive compensation program was no longer based on US standards, but was built as a global program with regional and country standards. This supported both the leadership initiative and the globalization initiative.

Dover has continued to build on its leadership initiative through its organizational development framework. Executive coaching programs have been added for key executive level positions in the company. Dover has also increased its commitment to formalization of its international assignments.

The Dover example is a positive story reminding us how important it is to examine the overall organizational development framework before shooting "silver bullets." Most of the time, there is no silver bullet. A well-integrated set of organizational development programs will serve to reinforce the HCI central to the business strategy and organizational goals.

While it's too early to tell if the Dover Leadership initiative will be successful in the long-term, from a distance it seems to be working. The company has a number of ways to measure the leadership initiative's success, but most telling will be whether or not the targeted number and/or percentage of top-level positions are filled from within.

A Big Picture View of Organizational Development

To conclude this chapter, I'd like to add some comments to support what has already been written.

First, as the Dover example shows, not all programs and initiatives can take place simultaneously. This is common sense, but many companies err on the side of trying to do too much. It often comes down to executives feeling that if they don't go fast and far enough, their companies will be outperformed. Only so much can be done according to the resources available, the management attention required, and the ability of the workforce to digest what has been served.

This doesn't mean programs should be introduced one at a time. It does mean that the organizational development framework should be examined comprehensively prior to a decision being made to go with any one program. By doing so, organizational leaders can make the best decisions about which programs to select and in what order.

Second, all the training programs of the company should be contemplated in the context of the organizational development framework, including those outside the responsibility of HR.

I will always remember a particular scenario when I was in charge of HR for Schlumberger's Test & Transactions group of companies. At the time, each function of the organization was charged with budgeting for their training activities and programs. There was a corporate training budget HR managed under my responsibility, but this was for programs sponsored by headquarters.

During this period, HSE ("health, safety, and environmental") had become a specific functional entity and had begun to provide HSE "required" training for all employees within the organization. Separately, the Information Technology function was a growing and changing entity, and training programs were being rolled out to help employees become more adept at using email and the Internet. The Marketing organization had product training activities needed to develop the commercial side of the business.

One afternoon during a quarterly executive staff meeting, one of the company's many training programs came to the attention of the senior management team. Realizing we had limited resources, each member of the executive team investigated the training programs taking place in each of our respective areas of responsibility. We then collected and analyzed the cost and time spent on all of the training programs in the company.

Upon completing this exercise, we were astonished by the findings. If we had invested in all of the planned training programs, the average employee would have spent well over six weeks of training away from his/her job, not to mention the costs associated with materials and external vendors, outside courses, and the like. Including the training time and external expenses, the total cost was probably over 12% of payroll, far over what even the best-in-class companies provide.

As you can imagine, this was a good lesson for us as an organization. It forced us to take a step back and think comprehensively. It also gave us the opportunity to think more strategically about our commitment to organizational development programs, and it forced us to do a better job of cross-functional planning. In the end, we reorganized our priorities to be in line with our business strategy and business goals, and then adjusted our spending and time management accordingly.

Every organization must decide for itself the level of commitment and investment it will make in training and development programs. The historical standard for determining an organization's training investment is "average number of training hours per employee." Some HR practitioners suggest that this is no longer a good metric since organizations change their training requirements from year to year based on a number of factors including business conditions and other organizational requirements. With the collection and analysis of data being much easier to facilitate because of advanced software technology, I believe that training metrics are still a proactive means for trending and review purposes.

For organizations serious about implementation of Human Capital Management, the commitment to build an organizational development framework that includes integrated training and development programs is a must. The companies most likely to succeed in leveraging their employees are those who invest in employee training to advance individual skills and those of the organization.

Along with "talent utilization," "organizational development" is the most powerful component within the performance wheel. With well-planned and well-managed design of an appropriate organizational development framework, it can stimulate personal and professional growth, engage employees to participate in organizational initiatives, be highly motivating, and increase the overall commitment of the organization. Understanding this, organizations need to increase the number and percentage of employees who have the opportunity to join task forces, committees, projects, and other teams. Ensuring RP@RP (right people in the right positions) and engaging the workforce through HCIs are critical components of Human Capital Management.

Chapter 14
The 3R's: Recognition, Rewards & Remuneration

In big business, much attention is given to monetary compensation, which includes a base salary and other cash or non-cash forms of compensation. The reality is that ever increasing, outlandish and over-the-top compensation schemes over the past twenty years or so have put this topic under the microscope. Compensation is a personal topic in a capitalistic society, so it's an emotional topic for most of us. For our employers, compensation accounts for a large percentage of an organization's costs. Perhaps then, compensation deserves the close attention and scrutiny it receives.

"Compensation" is the money earned for doing a particular job and "benefits" typically represent an in-kind value provided to the employee. While benefits can be costly and in the USA might represent roughly 25-30% of an employee's basic salary, they're usually not high motivators for employees. Unless there's a very specific benefit that happens to match an important need of an individual, it would be an exception for "benefits" to be a significant motivator.

Over the course of my career, I've closely observed the relationship between money and motivation of rank-and-file employees. What I've found to be most true is this: money isn't necessarily one of the most important motivators to individuals, but if the money or recognition for a job or performance is disproportionately lower than it should be, demotivation and dissatisfaction sets in.

In this chapter, we'll look at the most critical factors to motivate and influence behavior change from the 3R's: recognition, rewards, and remuneration. All can be used effectively (or not) in affecting the behavior of individuals.

Recognition: Underused and Undervalued

Based on my experience, very few executives excel at giving recognition. Perhaps executives and mid-level managers are too busy and pre-occupied to see the strains and challenges others need to overcome in completing projects. Sometimes the executives only see the outcome and not the hard work that goes into the project.

In the USA, "recognition" doesn't seem to be a tangible skill developed as a concept by itself. It seems we think about recognition as a verb "to recognize," not a "noun." Most of the time recognition is not planned. It's after the fact or spur of the moment. We realize someone did a good job. Therefore, we decide to offer a "pat on the back," and then walk away. Sometimes a "pat on the back" is more highly visible by holding a department meeting to congratulate an individual or team, but it's quick and fleeting.

What if executives and managers actually took recognition to another level as a formal approach to motivating people? **Imagine if we thought about individual and team milestones in advance, planning for appropriate recognition activities as motivators and reinforcements. This is the kind of recognition I'm advocating in Human Capital Management.**

Outside the USA, recognition needs to be handled carefully. In some countries, team recognition can be a motivator, while individual recognition can be frowned upon. Many American managers stumble on this cultural faux paux when visiting other countries. On more than one occasion I've seen American managers go into a country where individual praise is culturally taboo, and they go overboard in recognizing someone in front of their peers. When this happens, the individual receiving praise may actually feel badly, and the praise backfires. If the individual receives too much praise, he/she may feel a need to apologize to his or her teammates.

Recognition is constructive as a means to motivate people, but only if it's done sincerely and in the spirit of those being praised, not for the satisfaction of the appraiser. And it needs to be culturally suitable and appropriate.

To get into the habit of making recognition a standard part of your motivational tool kit, I recommend using the chart shown in Figure 17 below as a planning tool. For those of you who manage people directly, try it with your immediate direct reports and see what happens. I guarantee that it will make a noticeable difference in the motivation of your employees.

Figure 17

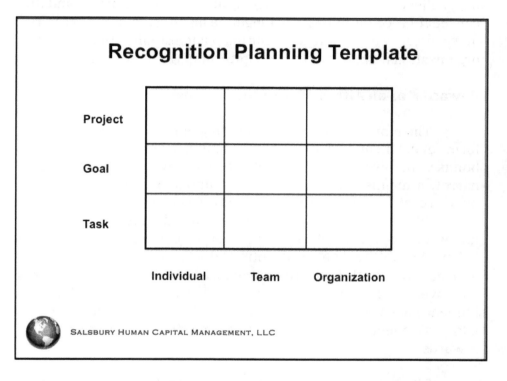

Think about one of your direct report's significant tasks, goals or projects they are assigned. These can be individual goals, team goals or organizational goals. The same holds true for tasks and projects. Obviously, the goals will be larger in scope from task to goal to project, and also from individual, to team, to organization. Considering the milestones established for the tasks, goals or projects, what would the appropriate recognition be for an individual, team or organization within your span of control? Why not list them in advance and modify them according to their individual level of success?

Many executives who are reading this may feel the idea of "recognition planning" is silly or to take the American expression "corny." Others may feel they don't have time for this kind of activity and prefer to wait until something good happens before thinking about recognition. And then there are those who think they're already masters at providing recognition and this approach may feel too structured. For those of you who fall into any of these categories, I invite you to try completing this matrix and use it just once. If you do, I believe you'll find your recognition skills will improve, and the concept of recognition will no longer be an afterthought. It's a very inexpensive way to motivate your team and establish the positive organizational mindset Human Capital Management seeks to create.

Rewards" as an Alternative to "Incentives"

The more common understanding of rewards includes all forms of payment, including compensation, incentives or other bonuses. In this chapter, I will refer specifically to a "reward" in a narrower manner as "something given unplanned and unexpected by the receiver to recognize effort and/or performance."

"Rewards" in the context of the above definition are underappreciated. Much ado is made of "incentives" since it's widely believed people will be more motivated when there is a bonus attached to goals. I'm an advocate of incentives for multiple levels of employees and believe they're effective levers for organizations to influence behavior. We will review incentives shortly when we address remuneration, but for now, let me share a story regarding rewards.

The earnings of many companies were dramatically impacted by the worldwide recession that began in late 2008. Very few companies were untouched, and Dover's Product Identification Group was no exception. One of its flagship organizations, Markem-Imaje, referred to earlier, was well on its way to achieving unprecedented growth until the global recession made its impact.

Despite the detailed and arduous budget planning that took place in the fall of 2008, it became apparent as soon as January 2009 that the budget would be virtually impossible to achieve with the slowdown in the world economy.

With short notice in January of 2009, Omar Kerbage, then-CEO of the Dover Product Identification Group, summoned his top 20 executives to Valence, France to review the options for recovery and build a plan to counteract revenue loss, at a minimum ensuring the company's profitability levels, despite the effects of the recession.

The two-day meeting was emotional and contentious as executives from around the world debated the level of cost cutting that could be made without creating negative long-term effects. Some couldn't understand why we simply didn't accept the loss of revenue and related loss of profitability as a consequence of the recession. While Kerbage knew the loss of revenue was inevitable, he insisted that management remain disciplined in maintaining a healthy operating income. Total profit dollars would be reduced as a direct correlation to loss of revenue, but reducing the profitability percentage was unacceptable. This was the standard of excellence the company had established in the past, and Omar refused to lower the standard of excellence that had taken time and effort to build.

2009 was quite a challenging year. Despite all of the efforts and execution of plans, the company's overall revenue did decline from the original budget plan. Yet, despite this decline, the company maintained its market share, and through good management and planning, its profitability levels.

Certainly these achievements were very difficult to accomplish. The actions taken to achieve a strong operating income required a hiring freeze, a refocus and reduction of engineering projects, and elimination of non-revenue creating activities. During it all, the workforce remained actively engaged and understood that this period of austerity was necessary. Despite fewer resources, longer working hours, and perhaps not as many company sponsored social activities, the workforce responded to the challenges given to them. They had done their part to fulfill their personal goals and the company's financial goals.

As the year came to a close, Omar and I began a discussion regarding our bonus programs for managers and employees. The incentive plan for managers, called the Management Bonus Plan was split with 50% of the bonus award based on financial results, and 50% of the bonus award based on personal goals. Another bonus program, called the USA Performance Bonus Plan, paid a bonus award to all US-based employees within the company contingent upon the company meeting its financial results.

As we discussed this topic, I reminded Omar of our bonus formula calculation, and the fact that our actual revenue achievement was below the minimum threshold to award a bonus for the portion based on the company's financial results. Therefore, for the Management Bonus Plan, the most a manager could receive would be 50% of the total bonus award. For those participating in the USA Performance Bonus Plan, there would be no bonus payout since the total payout was based on meeting the financial threshold.

Omar asked me how the workforce would react to not receiving the bonus portion based on financial results. In response, I described to him the different communications we had provided to managers and individual contributors throughout the year, keeping them updated regarding our financial performance and bonus tracking. They wouldn't expect to receive a bonus.

Omar then asked, "So despite achieving excellent operating income results, our workforce doesn't expect to receive a bonus?"

"Yes, that's right," I said.

Omar paused for a few seconds and replied, "We have to give them a reward. They deserve it. It's not their fault we didn't achieve our revenue target, but without them we wouldn't have achieved our operating income. Even though the incentive isn't completely achieved according to a bonus formula we devised, the performance is outstanding and deserves a reward."

The concept of providing a "reward" rather than an "incentive" wasn't new to me, yet my compensation and management training regarding incentives hadn't allowed me to comprehend this kind of logic. The idea of providing an award outside the incentive was even more disconcerting given all of the attention corporate governance had received regarding "pay for performance."

Omar continued, "perhaps we should give 50% to the managers for the financial performance with no upside, and be somewhat more stringent in our review of personal goals to be sure only those performing extremely well can achieve 100% of their total award target."

"Okay," I said, "but what about the USA Performance Bonus Plan? On what basis should we decide their reward amount?"

As if anticipating this question Omar said, "100% of the target award. We can get much more motivation and commitment for this coming year from our workforce if we show them the contribution for last year is a just reward, no matter what the incentive plan was. We need to respect the people."

And that was that. Omar informed other members of senior management of our intentions, and while there were questions and concerns offered no different than those I had shared with Omar, his courage and conviction to do the right thing was the deciding factor in providing a "reward" despite not meeting the "incentive" standards.

Now let's be clear. This kind of decision can't be taken on a regular basis. It has to be an exception and it has to be justifiable. It has to pass the litmus test of logic and business sense, and it has to have a purpose.

It's not simply about making people feel better about a difficult year or reinforcing a lousy performance culture by paying out an award regardless of business results. It has to connect to the overall values and desired culture. If it can be explained taking these factors into consideration, then it can be done. If the company hadn't been a high performance company, it wouldn't have achieved its operating income target. And if the company hadn't demonstrated a prior history of high-level performance, neither Omar nor Markem-Imaje would've had the credibility to provide a "reward."

"Rewards" are a type of recognition that is most often remembered and appreciated because it's least expected. As I look back on my own career, I remember the surprise rewards I received as much or more than I remember the ones I was expecting.

Remuneration: High Visibility and Overvalued

"Remuneration" is essentially compensation including all forms of payment, but I will limit its definition for this discussion to cash compensation in the form of base salary and cash bonuses. Remuneration as compensation gets much more visibility than either "recognition" or "rewards." However, there are many studies and articles suggesting compensation is no more motivating than other forms of recognition and rewards, and possibly less so.

Nonetheless, as part of the Human Capital Management System, compensation must be appropriately linked as part of the performance wheel to maximize the contribution of the workforce.

While executive and management compensation is an interesting topic receiving lots of attention, the Human Capital Management System is more concerned about the alignment of workforce compensation as a whole. In this regard, I would like to briefly address two of the most basic types of remuneration: base salary and "workforce" incentive bonuses.

A few years ago, I visited an underperforming company. As a result of weaknesses in the leadership team, the strategy and organizational goals of the company were numerous. Despite some well-qualified and skilled people in the organization, the company hadn't achieved financial success in a number of years.

As the company leadership did an assessment of its strategic needs, one of its conclusions was that the organization's skills needed to be upgraded to meet present and future needs. With this in mind, it was decided the HR organization would develop a competency based pay system, where a person's pay is linked to attainment of critical skills or knowledge.

As I listened to a few of the senior managers debrief me on the company's competitive situation, I reflected on the many issues and challenges they had to overcome to become successful. I wondered whether a competency based pay system was the right project for the company to pursue at the time, especially with the many challenges the company faced in the near-term just to break-even.

Whether or not a competency based pay system was appropriate in this situation is really not the point of this illustration though. More important, it's simply to make the point that all too often companies choose pay structure as one of the first areas to change when things aren't working right in other areas. Pay structures should be one of the last components for companies to work on. Once other key components of the performance wheel have been addressed, compensation programs should be reviewed for alignment.

Another example of the same type of compensation problem occurred with the advent of "solutions" companies that came into popularity during the decade of the 90's. Instead of spending time on redefining roles and responsibilities separating product sales people from solutions sales people, companies frequently reacted by redefining the pay structure. More often than not, this added to the level of confusion between product and solutions sales, and in some cases, cost of sales actually went up, not down.

So when is it reasonable to review and make significant changes in compensation structures?

When the pay structure of an organization is no longer aligned with the business foundation or business strategy it should be reviewed. Pay structures should be carefully assessed in view of the organizational goals and the other spokes in the performance wheel as well. They should reflect the culture of the company and how people are expected to work. For high performance cultures where people and their pay are separated by performance, "merit pay" and "pay for performance" work extremely well. For organizations where employees need to be flexible and move from one area to another based on company requirements, "skill based pay" might be more applicable.

For international companies, management needs to be careful with how it applies its compensation and recognition policies. In various countries around the world, going with pure "merit" based pay increases is against business practices and in some cases it's illegal to only give salary raises based on merit. This makes the drive towards global practices and a common worldwide culture more difficult to put in place. It can also create challenges for managers who have employees in multiple countries. Sometimes a lack of international experience can incorrectly result in managers using their own country's standard in establishing pay policies and practices for those they manage outside their own country.

The proper utilization of pay programs is essential whether we're speaking of base pay, salary increases or incentive structures. Companies should be careful to respect local country cultures, practices, and regulations while seeking to drive a consistent approach to support the business foundation and business strategy to the extent practical and possible.

You may recall the story I told earlier of Markem Corporation and its transition starting in 2002 from a paternalistic culture to a higher-level performance culture.

When I first joined Markem Corporation in 2001, the company had just provided the workforce with a holiday bonus. There were no incentive criteria for the bonus. In fact, the bonus was given at the sole discretion of the ownership and management of the company. Over the years, when the company's financial results for the year were forecast to be good, senior management was gracious and kind enough to deliver part of this payment before Thanksgiving so employees could spend it for holiday shopping. Pending the final results for the year, the company would make a payment for the remainder of the bonus in the first quarter. It was a benefit that was much appreciated by the workforce. After awhile, employees throughout the company came to expect the payment and took it for granted that the holiday bonus would be provided regardless of the company's financial position.

In 2002, the company's position on the holiday bonus changed. With the results of the company at lower levels than expected, in October we announced to our workforce that there would be no holiday bonus. Then we did something most unusual. We announced to the workforce that we would pay the bonus six months later pending satisfactory financial results. In other words, if our financial results were strong in the first half of 2003, we would pay the 2002 holiday bonus halfway into the 2003-year.

Next, we announced that the traditional holiday bonus was being eliminated and being replaced with a "performance bonus" for the 2003 plan year. Rather than leave them guessing as to the amount they could earn, a bonus formula was put together merging revenue and operating income. If the company achieved 100% of its revenue and 100% of its operating income, the payout of the performance bonus would be at 100% or 40 hours of pay. If the company achieved much higher levels of revenue and operating income, the payment could go as high as 80 hours of pay. If the financial results were below the minimum threshold established, there would be no bonus payout.

The workforce was not thrilled that the holiday bonus was going away and being replaced with the performance bonus, but they appreciated the transparency of management. For the most part, they understood this replacement program gave them an opportunity to earn more than what they had earned in the past, but with some risk as well.

As the first half of 2003 unfolded, the company's financial results improved dramatically. While the company was not fully back to profit levels of past years, the financial results warranted payback of the 2002 bonus that hadn't been paid. Shortly after the first half of the year ended, a communications meeting was organized for the 600 headquarters employees to attend. In addition to explaining to employees that they would receive a check for the 2002 bonus, we also thanked them for their hard work and patience during a difficult financial period. For this we informed them that each employee would receive an additional day of paid time-off to be taken before the end of the year. This day off was a "reward" and given out of appreciation for their willingness to accept and embrace the performance culture changes in the company. As you can imagine, this approach paid dividends with our workforce, both in terms of motivation and trust.

The 3R's of "recognition, rewards, and remuneration" are complementary tools that make up an important spoke in the performance wheel. Normally, the 3R's shouldn't be utilized as HCIs in the center of the performance wheel. When this occurs, management is trying to use extrinsic rewards as the primary motivator, and more often than not, this is short-lived and superficial. Instead these tools should be linked to the business foundation, business strategy, and the other components of the performance wheel.

Chapter 15
Internal Communications:
Formalizing a Plan is a Must

If a company's values are the "glue" that holds the organization together, then "internal communications" are the reinforcements to ensure that the different components of the Human Capital Management System are complementary and support one another. In this regard, it's incumbent upon management to keep the workforce well informed.

The idea of leveraging the workforce for a competitive advantage shouldn't be a secret or something for management to be embarrassed about. Part of this success formula is to make sure the workforce understands its role as a differentiator.

Therefore, management must educate and explain the practice and concepts of Human Capital Management to the workforce. Coupled with this should be a straightforward explanation of how the elements of the system come together.

Some skeptics might challenge the notion of explaining the inner workings of the Human Capital Management System to the workforce.

"Is this really necessary?" they might ask. My answer is an emphatic "Yes!"

Here's why.

First, in a Human Capital Management organization, the most valuable asset is the workforce itself. A level of trust and respect must be developed so the employees take their role seriously and with great pride. People are smarter and more trustworthy than we often give them credit for. When management says employees are their greatest assets, they need to show it through their actions. This includes the full explanation about how the workforce will be deployed as a competitive advantage. Otherwise, the idea is only a concept, and the skeptics will appear.

Communicating about the Human Capital Management System has side benefits that support the quality of operations. Continuous and consistent communications reinforcing Human Capital Management principles serve as reminders to management of the high standard and commitment the organization has signed up for. Managers must live up to these standards as they perform in their roles. After all, for employees to be energized and motivated, managers must be facilitators within the system, not detractors. When employees are continually reminded of the importance of the workforce as part of the overall business culture and strategy, they're more likely to question and challenge poor management representatives and actions. For sincere senior managers who care about good management techniques and practices, this built-in, bottom-up approach to quality control should be welcome.

Finally, as employees are made aware of the critical role of the workforce and how the Human Capital Management System is supposed to function, they will be more likely to flag operational issues and inconsistencies when they arise. This is beneficial given the many different moving parts within the system itself. Fully engaged employees will be more likely to become proactive in identifying inconsistencies in policies they deal with on a day-to-day basis when these inconsistencies are overlooked by management.

To summarize, the implementation of a Human Capital Management System needs to include an open and direct understanding with the workforce that it's the most valuable asset of the organization. Employees should be partners in the process, not pawns to be manipulated.

Who Owns Internal Communications in Human Capital Management?

Most of the for-profit companies I'm familiar with don't have stand-alone Communications Departments. Very large businesses or organizations exposed to the public may be exceptions to this rule. In small companies, the Marketing department or HR might handle internal communications responsibilities. In midsize companies, internal communications responsibilities might fall between Marketing Communications and HR. In larger corporations, internal communications responsibilities might be split between a corporate Communications function and its subsidiaries. It's possible your organization has a different setup.

Internal communications responsibilities normally include determination of the right communication forum to deliver messages to the workforce or segments of the workforce. These can take place in many different forms such as management meetings, written memos or announcements, and bulletin board postings either onsite or via the intranet.

For a Human Capital Management System to be successful, it requires a determination of who owns what type of internal communication. When it's unclear who owns internal communications, assemble a cross-functional team of people from those areas within the organization that traditionally have some internal communications role. The sponsor of the team should be a member of senior management who is unbiased and has a vested interest in ensuring proper definition of roles. Then work on establishing levels of responsibility.

In establishing an internal communications structure, there are a number of key questions that should be addressed for each communications activity, including:

- What is the communication topic? (Example: organizational announcement)

- What is the means of communication and how will it be communicated?
  (Example: organizational announcement by intranet, written document posted on electronic or building bulletin boards)

- What is the communications process from start to finish? (Example: when someone gets promoted, who has responsibility to start the communications process, who approves it, who sends it and receives it, and so on?)

- What is the scope of communications responsibilities? (Example: is it a local site, regional, functional or organization-wide announcement?)

- Will the communication be in English or will it need to be made in the local language? How will this be determined?

Companies should also consider cross-functional areas where more than one function has responsibility for communications actions. For example, it may be the responsibility of Marketing Communications to create a video for external use with customers or to build an external brand. Certainly, the HR team should be engaged early in the process to ensure there is agreement regarding key messaging in the video, and with the internal employment brand.

As part of the effort to build a strong and consistent internal communications structure to support the Human Capital Management System, each of the "elements" of the system should be evaluated to determine communications responsibilities. For example, whose role will it be to build communications for the company values and the company culture? How will the organizational strategy be communicated, and what about the organizational goals coming from the strategy? When an HCI such as lean management is developed, what function will have the responsibility for communicating it? All of the elements of the Human Capital Management System need to be carefully reviewed for consistency, and to identify in advance any potential gaps or overlaps in communication.

Internal Communications Plans Should be Standard Operating Procedure

Ongoing communications activities can take place efficiently and effectively once internal communications roles and responsibilities have been established within the organization.

More action is required, however, to guarantee a well-informed workforce. Next comes the development of an internal communications plan. Unfortunately, very few companies actually create written internal communications plans. When the HR, Marketing or Marketing Communications functions have responsibility for internal communications, they are often too busy working on their core functional responsibilities and goals to pay attention to creation of an internal communications plan. Nevertheless, communications can be managed more professionally and proactively when such a plan is written.

The internal communications plan starts with a review of the business foundation. In this regard, is the mission and vision clear or are they unknown to the general employee population? How well entrenched are the values and culture of the company? Is there a need to revisit company culture? Answering these types of questions will help determine whether or not communications regarding the business foundation need to be addressed.

There's always a need to reinforce the business foundation. I recommend specific and dedicated communications take place annually for this purpose. The business strategy and related annual goals and initiatives of the organization should be communicated as well. In many organizations, the strategy is revisited on a rolling three-year basis, and then goals are set for the upcoming year based on the updated strategy. Functional strategies and goals should be communicated in the annual communication plan as well. In particular, internal communications should highlight the relationship of HCIs with other organizational goals.

Clarity and consistency of communications are vital to successful Human Capital Management. Taking the time to develop and execute an internal communications plan annually will undoubtedly lead to a well-informed workforce who understands its role within the complete Human Capital Management System.

Section 4
Putting it all Together

At this point, you should have a good understanding of the Human Capital Management System, and how each element of the system, and each component within the performance wheel are integrated for maximum impact. By aligning the business strategy to the business foundation, and then developing organizational goals via the spokes in the performance wheel, your Human Capital Management System is ready to be operational.

As a minimum, an organization that follows the Human Capital Management roadmap will improve its efficiency and effectiveness. However, for organizations that believe in the power of human capital, and intend to leverage their people as a competitive advantage beyond operational efficiencies, there are a couple more ingredients to add to the success recipe.

The first of these ingredients is "active leadership" in the organization, specifically related to the implementation of HCIs. As I've said before, the workforce can be utilized as a competitive advantage only if top leadership communicates and demonstrates its commitment to this end. An HCI may be only one of the organizational goals, but in order for a workforce mobilization to occur, the overriding principle must be that people are the primary asset of the organization. A "process" oriented company with a culture centered on business process improvements and lean management can utilize people to achieve an HCI, but when the initiative is complete the company will still be a "process improvement" company. If we take the example in reverse, a "human capital management" company working on a process improvement initiative will look at the project from a perspective based on human capital principles. At the end of the improvement initiative, the company culture will remain human capital based.

A company can only excel at Human Capital Management with active leadership centered on human capital. We'll review this in Chapter 16 where we'll examine leadership principles from the perspective of a CEO.

Certainly leadership extends beyond the CEO position within an organization, and typically includes the top management team that reports to the CEO. All those on the management team must drink from the human capital cup for the organization to truly reflect a people driven organizational culture. For Human Capital Management to take hold though, there is one particular function that deserves more discussion than the rest, which is, the Human Resources role. Even though Human Capital Management is an organization-wide practice, the HR function is the best placed function within the organization to be the operational backbone for its implementation. The nature of HR's roles and responsibilities make it a logical choice to be front and center in becoming the functional advocate and active proponent of Human Capital Management. For this reason, we'll review HR's role in Chapter 17.

With these added ingredients, Human Capital Management can roll forward with the momentum needed to sustain itself through difficult periods in a company's life cycle.

Chapter 16
Leadership – A Critical Ingredient for the Human Capital Management System to Work Effectively

When I was a young professional and a first-level manager, my views about senior management were pretty naïve. From my earliest encounters with company Presidents and CEOs, I was in awe of their rich knowledge of the subjects they chose to speak about, and amazed by how broad-based their skills seemed to be. During those years, my uninformed belief was that to become an effective company President, one would need a wide range of business and leadership skills.

Based on what I've learned and observed over the years since, in my opinion and with no disrespect intended, there are very few Presidents or CEOs with a wide range of strong, comprehensive business and leadership skills. This view has been formulated by 30+ years in business, and based on having worked directly for a number of Presidents/CEOs and General Managers over the course of my career.

Let me explain in further detail.

Rising up in the management ranks of a company is a little bit like growing up. As young children we look up to our parents through rose-colored glasses. As kids, we think they can do no wrong. They're older and wiser than we are, and it seems as though they have all the right answers when we need them. As we grow into our teens and think for ourselves, we begin to question the wisdom of our parents and the decisions they make or have made.

It's a painful realization for kids when they discover their parents aren't perfect (It's painful for the parents too!). As adults, most of us understand it's our imperfections that cause children to question our judgment, and this logically causes them to feel like they're ready to make their own decisions.

As first-line managers grow into mid-level managers, and mid-level managers grow into senior managers, they begin to see that those in top leadership positions have their flaws as well. As people get to higher levels of management, CEO flaws and mistakes become much more exposed to the people who have direct access to the corporate suite on a regular basis.

I'm not suggesting CEOs lack the right expertise and experience to be successful in their jobs. On the contrary, I've found that the majority of CEOs I've worked for or with to be very capable business leaders. What I'm suggesting is that the top leaders of organizations have strengths and weaknesses representative of their backgrounds. They shouldn't be expected to have skills reaching beyond their own expertise and experiences.

One of the problems many leaders face is that they're sometimes expected by their constituents (shareholders, board members, subordinates, Wall Street analysts, rank and file employees) to have an unlimited set of skills. This is why the job of the chief executive isn't for the faint of heart.

No matter how strong their backgrounds are, at some point in their tenure as a CEO, they will encounter unknown or unforeseen problems and challenges. This is logical since the issues a CEO has to deal with are amazingly wide-ranging.

In many cases, they won't respond appropriately given gaps in their skills sets. Leaders who fall into this category often suffer from certain traits or characteristics that are manifested in the way they operate.

Here are just a few examples you may recognize from your own experiences being a CEO or working for CEOs (or other senior managers at high levels in an organization):

- **Most Presidents and CEOs are very good at a few "functional" skills, and likewise, they are typically not so good at some other functional skills.** For example, I've found it's rare for top executives who come from Finance career backgrounds to be experts in Sales and Marketing. Likewise, those in Sales and Marketing aren't typically knowledgeable in Manufacturing. CEOs can gain expertise in improving multi-functional skills with time and experience in the job, but it's not so easy. The nature of the CEO's job requires time be spent on many different subjects, and the time (and interest) required to be an expert in any one functional skill area is significant.

- Many people assume CEOs have been promoted throughout their careers because they're good decision-makers and have been right the majority of the time. For some executives, this may be true, but for others this isn't necessarily the case. There are multiple reasons and stories behind how and why people have grown through management ranks to top positions. I know of no companies keeping track of the good/bad decision ratio or weighted scores of their executives' decision-making. It's probably more likely that promotions take place when a number of key factors come together at the same time. The rationale for the selection of top executives is often due to certain leadership characteristics fitting with the company's culture, and the CEO may have managed high profile projects that were deemed successful. In some companies, as long as the person has the right cultural attributes, and doesn't make major career mistakes along the way, "hanging around" long enough without getting fired can lead to promotions. There are plenty of CEOs who have failed in one position, only to be hired for a top position with another company. In some cases, CEOs may have a tendency to think they're right even when their skill level and decision-making capabilities aren't sufficient. Often their subordinates can see these deficiencies, but are powerless to do much about it.

- **The best CEO is one who is a good "manager" and a good "leader," but I've seen several cases where the CEO is one or the other, but not both.** It's a real problem when a Chief Executive Officer believes he/she is both a strong manager and leader, when one of these skills is weak. Imagine the mess caused by an energetic and enthusiastic leader who is capable of firing up the troops to follow his strategic direction, but who struggles to manage implementation properly because he/she isn't a good manager. I've seen this occur multiple times and the result is usually poor execution. You may find other examples through your own experiences that are similar to those listed above.

- The best CEOs don't necessarily need personal expertise or past experiences to handle many issues coming their way. They don't typically suffer the characteristics pointed out by the examples above. **True leaders have the capability to understand they don't need to be experts at everything. They don't have to be right all the time. They recognize their own strengths and weaknesses. They realize that they have multiple resources at their fingertips to address a myriad of issues where they don't have specific expertise themselves.** The best CEOs are comfortable with who they are, and treat all their constituencies, from board members to rank-and-file employees with respect and courtesy.

To be an effective CEO capable of driving an organization to achieve great things, it's necessary to have "human capital leadership" capabilities. Executives who have a shortage of such capabilities will have difficulty mobilizing the workforce. Similarly, the higher level of human capital leadership skills a CEO has, the more that people will follow. This is human nature, and a basic principle of Human Capital Management.

The most important prerequisite to building an organization that wishes to utilize its people effectively is strong leadership and support of Human Capital Management from the CEO. With it, the impact of a human capital program can be powerful and game changing for an organization. Without it, even the best conceived human capital programs will more than likely fizzle out before they gain any organizational traction. The most valuable books and articles written about leadership don't speak of leadership traits alone. They focus on examples showing leadership in action, and provide practical guidance.

Let me share with you what I believe to be the most important leadership principles to be followed when implementing HCIs.

Leadership Principles Required in Human Capital Management

1) Value Employees as Your #1 Asset

Top leaders must believe the workforce can offer a substantial competitive advantage, but believing is not enough. The leadership concept of Human Capital Management carries a responsibility to understand that there's a cause and effect relationship between the way employees are treated, and how they will treat their customers. When employees are content and motivated, they enjoy the challenges of their jobs, the relationship with their managers, the potential they have for career growth, open communication channels, and so on. **In Human Capital Management companies, leaders show their employees through their actions that they understand and respect the value of the workforce.**

2) Hire Great People and Trust Them to do Their Jobs

Top leaders hire good people and utilize them for the skills and capabilities for which they were hired. At one company where I worked, one of my peers warned me in the early days of my employment that the company undervalued its executives and overvalued the advice of consultants. He joked with me that I should push my views and ideas as much as possible in the first six months of being hired. He said that afterwards, the honeymoon would be over, and I would no longer have the "he knows something we don't know" aura. To a certain extent, he was right. As I assimilated into the team, I noticed the CEO had a tendency to retain external consultants for projects or decisions for many diverse topics in all areas of the business that could've easily been managed in-house. As time went on, I learned that this approach was a deeply imbedded cultural attribute of the company, and it had been this way for decades. This was an unfortunate waste of time and money, not to mention a de-motivator to the executive team. It was illogical to hire senior executives to manage an operation, and then regularly hire consultants to validate or challenge those decisions as a normal course of business.

There is nothing wrong with bringing in a consultant to help out in areas where there is a lack of internal expertise. The same logic applies to asking board members for their advice. However, these types of resources can be overused. **Hire great people and trust them by seeking out their advice, expertise, and experience. Unless there is some reason to doubt the capability or performance of senior management, they know their functional expertise, the industry and/or the company better than what an outside consultant can bring.** In my experience, consultants should complement or add value to what management can bring, not act as a replacement for management.

3) The Chief Must Own It

The willingness of the Chief Executive Officer to get in front of an HCI and push it directly and personally is a prerequisite for success. "Owning" an HCI doesn't mean making a nice speech about the need for the organization to pursue it and then moving on to what the CEO thinks is a more important matter. **The CEO needs to spend the necessary time working with other key executives to flesh out the ideas, challenges, and potential problems of an initiative before it's launched. This ownership includes building support within the senior management team to ensure they're on board as well. Lastly, it includes consistent and continuous actions and follow through during the life of the initiative to demonstrate participative leadership, and as important, to build and sustain momentum within the organization.**

Unfortunately, this doesn't always happen for a variety of reasons and here are a few:

- The CEO may not be fully committed to the initiative, and wants to see how well it goes before he/she puts his support behind it.

- The CEO is preoccupied with other priorities and doesn't feel he/she has the time to invest in all of them.

- The CEO feels comfortable in certain areas of involvement, and others are off-limits. For example, some CEOs are not comfortable dealing with IT issues, and therefore, ask their CFO to manage this function. Many times they will do so for "span of control" reasons.

I've seen numerous cases throughout my career where CEOs have demonstrated a tremendous amount of leadership in actively leading and supporting HCIs. In every one of these cases where the CEO's leadership was apparent, the senior management team and the workforce were fired up and motivated to accomplish great things.

Among my favorite stories of the "the chief owning it," is one involving Irwin Pfister, who was Group President at the time and soon after became CEO of SchlumbergerSema. The company was comprised of a number of divisions, and for the purpose of simplicity, we'll call each of these companies "business operations." These business operations were organized functionally, with all of the business functions of each operation reporting directly to the President of the business.

During this period, many businesses across the United States had decided to evolve from "products" companies to "solutions" companies. Instead of simply selling a range of products, solutions companies often provide a variety of integrated hardware and software products and services. Conceptually, solutions companies achieve better profit margins than product companies. Theoretically at least, they are able to get closer to their customers because they offer solutions that place them higher up in the value chain.

Like these companies, it was our intention to transform from a products company to a solutions company. This would require many different actions, and among them was restructuring the organization.

What was formerly a traditional "functional" organization structure would be split into a hybrid organization structure consisting of "product" operations and "regional" operations. The product groups would be responsible for product marketing, engineering design, quality, and the overall P&L of the product line. The regional groups would be responsible for sales, service, applications support, and field marketing, as well as other customer facing functions. There would be two Product Presidents and four Regional Presidents, and a Vice President of Manufacturing Operations. These executive positions, as well as executive staff functions, including mine as the senior worldwide HR leader, would report directly to the President of the Group.

There were many complexities to this change. One of the most critical was that the internal roles and responsibilities ("R&R's") within the organization would need to be reworked and then communicated to the workforce. For example, the process used in establishing pricing policies would need to be modified to reflect the new hybrid organization and in consideration of revised R&R's. This was also true for other processes such as product launches, determination of product portfolios, and sales discount policies, to name a few.

Irv knew that communicating the organizational change itself wouldn't be enough. There needed to be multiple and sustained efforts to help the organization make a successful transition from being a products company to a solutions company. A full-scale effort was required to align the internal operations of the organization so they worked as intended. This needed to be done seamlessly and transparently, and in a manner to serve our customers more effectively, giving us the potential to generate additional revenues.

Irv also understood the operational impact of this change on the internal workings of the business. Knowing we couldn't let these internal changes impact our ability to serve our customers, he branded the initiative as the "Customer Focus Program." By choosing this name, it was his intention to keep the customer at the center of our focus as we painstakingly reviewed our internal R&R's and key business processes. His role in "owning" the initiative was never in doubt.

The Customer Focus Program (CFP) consisted of a number of complementary sub-initiatives intended to reinforce one another and the overall theme of improved customer focus and satisfaction. While all of them won't be examined here, I want to highlight a few of them that were crucial to our efforts. The following examples show how leadership plays an essential role in the implementation of an HCI.

4) The CEO Can't Do It All Alone

Irv recognized that it would be important to enlist the support of the senior executive team. While almost all of those in the C-suite were directly impacted, most would continue to remain on the executive team, even if their roles and titles would change with the revised organizational structure. Organizational changes impacting senior executives shouldn't be taken lightly. Most executive positions are very visible to the organization, and an unhappy senior executive can become very contagious with others on the team. If the senior leaders become dissatisfied with the changes being made, poor morale trickles down through the organization.

Irv scheduled a two-day meeting to be held at our corporate headquarters in Manhattan. Since he had personally briefed each member of the executive team individually prior to the meeting, this was to be a working meeting where the executive team would outline the key topics needing to be addressed. Irv's approach was both autocratic and democratic. He was autocratic in his insistence on maintaining the key principles of the new organizational structure and who would have responsibility for what. He was democratic in allowing the executive team to work through the details of each principle and decision encountered. He stepped in and acted as a referee, offering his advice, and in some cases taking the decision himself only when necessary, and usually after disagreements became animated.

The meeting in New York was an important first step. It gave Irv the opportunity to engage the senior management team, and let them swim around in the pond together while digesting the magnitude of the changes being thrust on them. No doubt it helped some of them accept the changes knowing their colleagues were in the same position as themselves. Additionally, the meeting provided Irv with a forum to re-bond the executive team as some of them contemplated new roles in the company. At the conclusion of the meeting, each member of the team felt like a contributor to the future roadmap since we strategized many of the key decisions together.

5) The Message from the Chief Must be Clear and Compelling

Shortly after the executive team met in New York, Irv and I did a communications tour of our key locations around the world to explain the rationale behind the organizational changes, and why we were making them. We put together a PowerPoint presentation accompanied by a "Questions and Answers" document and backup slides to provide as much readily available information as possible. Then, we made our way to the major offices around the world to communicate the changes.

In each location, we gathered our management teams and Irv started the meeting by explaining in detail why the changes had taken place, what the intended outcomes were, and the plans for implementation. Following Irv's review of the fundamental aspects of the changes, I presented the new organization charts, explaining who was in which role, and what the responsibilities were for different functions within the new hybrid organization structure.

Each meeting lasted about 90 minutes including questions and answers, but we were prepared to spend as much time as necessary with our employees to make sure they were comfortable with all of the concepts presented. After the meetings were concluded, Irv and I lingered so managers with specific questions could approach us individually. This added about another hour to the meetings. Our world tour covered several cities in a short period of time so that employees all over the world heard the messages on a timely basis.

There were a number of positive outcomes that came from these communications, in addition to a few lessons to be learned.

First, I'll give you a few of the positives:

- Face to face communication from the chief can be a compelling form of communication since there are no intermediaries. This increases the chances for information to be communicated as intended.

- Taking the time to allow individuals to meet with us privately was important to those who still had questions after the presentations.

- The meetings gave Irv and I the opportunity to provide information, and to ask questions and gather information we would eventually use to help us improve our communication/presentations going forward.

A few of the lessons that we benefited from included the following:

- What was "clear and compelling" to senior management was not necessarily "clear and compelling" to the managers we presented to. Irv and I had been working on this re-organization for weeks, and much of what we presented, we took for granted what we already understood and our managers didn't. Perhaps we should've tried a pilot session with a group of managers or even individual contributors to check on whether the information was received as intended.

- Nationalities and ethnic groups receive information and provide their own feedback in very different ways. In a few instances, we received more feedback and questions passed on to us from senior managers of a location outside the USA after we had left the city. Mid-level managers in some countries were too respectful to ask challenging questions or give us direct feedback. They went to their immediate superiors instead.

- There were "hot spots" within the organization we should've anticipated. These were places where the changes wouldn't necessarily be easy or where some managers weren't as strong in supporting the restructure as we'd expected.

Upon returning to our New York headquarters, Irv and I regrouped to examine the overall effectiveness of our communications tour, and we knew there was still work ahead of us to complete a successful reorganization.

6) The CEO Must Enable the Workforce

One afternoon shortly after returning to New York, Irv and I met in his office to brainstorm ideas for driving the Customer Focus Program initiative. By this time, we had gathered feedback from our worldwide communications tour and solicited input from other members of Irv's executive team.

In summary, here are the deliverables that came from this meeting:

- We would develop a specific training program for all employees in the company. For professional and managerial employees, these sessions would be two-day training sessions, and for manufacturing and service workers, they would be half-day sessions, as we needed to keep our production operations going.

- The training course would include the following key ingredients:

  o We would provide an introductory review session of the "why we did this," "what it means for the company," and "what it means for you." This would include a review of the organizational structure as well as detailed roles and responsibilities. All the senior leaders of the organization would be scheduled to make this part of the presentation according to their location, and according to the number of sessions we planned to hold.

  o We would build a total of six case studies, and use three of these in each program session. Each of the case studies would focus on our core internal operations processes, and how the roles and responsibilities of those involved in the processes would be different under the new organizational structure. We would pick the three most applicable case studies according to the mix of the participants in the respective training sessions. We would provide flow charts outlining the key business processes within the internal workings of the organization, and show roles and responsibilities for each process step and decision.

o   Realizing many employees wouldn't be experts in "flow charting" and "process management," we appointed a mid-level manager from the Quality function of the organization to design a training presentation on "process management." This presentation would become part of the two-day training program.

Remembering the lessons learned from our world tour, Irv and I then decided to run a pilot program. But instead of asking senior managers or mid-managers to attend, we invited a group of 25 high potential employees from all over the world to attend a dress rehearsal of the Customer Focus Program. Irv presented the first section of the program, and then we brought a few other senior executives in to moderate the case studies section. The manager who designed the process management section also presented his piece.

Prior to launching the program throughout the company, we scheduled a handful of sessions to train a number of "champions" as facilitators for the Customer Focus Program. These individuals were selected from every function and key location throughout the company. These were well-respected people who had potential to grow within the company, and would have the enthusiasm and energy to assist top management in driving this HCI successfully. It was motivating to those who were selected to know we had the confidence in them to be leaders of a major company program.

The commitment to build momentum through training and involvement of the workforce can't be underestimated. Some CEOs believe their employees will accept whatever comes down the pike, but the best ones know there is a significant

difference in the impact of an HCI when there is enthusiasm vs. disgruntlement. Leadership is the difference.

7) Lead by Example: "Walk the Talk"

The best part about the Customer Focus Program was that Irv was adamant that the Presidents and other senior executives reporting directly to him should write the case studies. We matched up members of Irv's executive staff in accordance with the case studies they were best suited to write, then Irv called another meeting with the purpose of informing them of their assignments. In doing so, he explained they would be asked to collaborate in small teams to write the case studies, with the assistance of additional designated subject-expert subordinates. They would also need to design the updated business processes to accompany the case studies. Upon initially hearing that Irv expected them to actually write the case studies and design the business processes and flow charts themselves, the senior team was incredulous. However, their disbelief was quickly made a reality when Irv read to them the teams he had decided were going to work together. To help them get started and push the process along, we then scheduled a two-day work session where we would all meet together off-site and begin the arduous work of writing the case studies and designing the processes. Deadlines were established for the cases to be polished up and completed two weeks later, and for the most part, everyone delivered on their commitments.

Upon completion of the case studies, the senior team met once again to review them together. The senior executives who developed each of the case studies and processes guided the rest of us through the materials, and this led to further discussion and debate, editing, and refinement. At the same meeting, we organized a video shoot where an outside firm came in and interviewed each of the senior executives regarding the business model and organizational structure. This would be used as an additional medium to communicate and reinforce our messaging and also served as marketing material.

This approach paid big dividends with our senior management team. To start with, since they had written the case studies and designed the business processes themselves, they were fully committed to the training. Second, the development process gave them the opportunity to better understand how Irv saw the organization working. It further enabled them to become ambassadors for the program. They were in a better position to coach and encourage employees, and persuade them when necessary that the changes being made were the right steps for our organizational evolution.

Looking back on this change from a functional to a hybrid organizational structure, it's difficult (even with program metrics) to assess whether or not our businesses benefited. Our revenues and net income continued to increase, but solutions revenue came slowly and incrementally. There are two overall conclusions that I'm confident of though. First, our employees were well educated and prepared for the changes being made via the multi-dimensional and repeated communications and training provided. Second, the adaptation of the redefined business processes allowed our employees to continue to provide customers with quality products and services delivered on time, while also dealing with internal changes.

8) The CEO Needs to Set Expectations and Hold People Accountable

Any organization committed to excellence sets goals for itself, each function or department, teams and/or individuals. Each of these goals should be tracked and measured. In today's business world, there are numerous sophisticated measurement tools organizations can use to measure their goals. Some companies prefer the "bowling scorecard" approach, which typically requires monthly or even weekly updates on the progress of goals. Another popular approach is the "dashboard," where the most important organizational metrics are tracked and visually shown in a simple, easy to read format.

While I strongly believe in the use of metrics, I don't believe there is much use in holding weekly or monthly meetings for the sole purpose to review the metrics themselves. There are plenty of ways to provide updates and accountability without having to schedule these types of meetings. I do believe meetings are useful with subordinates for "milestone reviews" where approval or validation needs to occur before a project moves on to the next stage. I also believe in meetings with subordinates where a manager can provide mentoring, advice, counseling or redirection. These are most valuable when the manager is actually adding value to the subordinate by offering experiential advice rather than simply keeping score. Whatever way a CEO decides to set and track goals with his/her subordinates, the role of the CEO should be much more than to simply review progress against results.

The CEO's job in setting expectations and holding people accountable is not just about metrics. It's also about developing and maintaining a "spirit of commitment" standard. Too many CEOs think their subordinates and rank-and-file employees will follow their direction without question. It may be true that a percentage of the workforce will in fact do this. However, there is also a percentage of the organization that needs to be convinced an HCI deserves their commitment. Once the CEO and his/her team have done their job by providing clear and compelling messaging about the initiative, they need to provide equally clear messaging regarding the expected behavior and/or actions needed to follow.

Human Capital projects involve topics where people are at the center of the activity. They aren't highly technical in nature. They're subjects where it's easy to have an opinion about whether the project will generate the kind of results expected. By nature, human capital projects are difficult to measure since it's a challenge to find a direct correlation between the results of the HCI and high-level financial results. People within an organization may question whether an HCI is worthwhile. For this reason, it's particularly important to establish accountability standards.

Let's revisit the story of lean management at Markem that I referred to earlier in Chapter 11. I first learned about the concept of lean management from one of our senior Manufacturing executives, who had become tremendously enthusiastic about it. Convinced lean management would bring significant value to the company, he was successful in persuading a few senior managers that we should go to a seminar being held on the topic. Three senior managers attended the seminar, hosted by the Manufacturing executive as our sponsor.

After having attended the seminar, our conclusion was that Markem would benefit enormously from lean management. Shortly thereafter, a meeting was organized with the senior management team to discuss further pursuit of lean implementation as a part of our business strategy.

The management team personally led the effort to drive lean management as an HCI. Training was organized for the senior executive team at our headquarters location, and soon after, it was added as an important element of our business strategy. As kaizen events were organized, the senior managers participated as team members. Each of the lean or kaizen events started early on Monday morning and went well into the evening, ending on Friday mornings when there were "report-outs" to the organization. These report-outs were short verbal reports of the team's progress during the week including a review of productivity improvements the teams came up with.

Not everyone in the company was in favor of lean management at Markem. After all, if lean was successful, there would be significant cost reductions and efficiencies in operations. Productivity improvements would eliminate jobs.

The "Redeployment Policy" shown in Chapter 11 was put in place to reassure employees that even if they were displaced by a productivity improvement resulting from a lean event, they would remain with the company and be placed in another job. Despite this policy, there were still detractors. Some were upfront and blatant in their criticisms, others were less public about it, but nonetheless worked behind the scenes to discredit the program.

While good progress was being made, management expected everyone in the organization would get on board. One day in a company-wide communications meeting, one of the senior managers matter-of-factly announced that everyone in the organization needed to support this initiative. An alternative choice was to leave the company. There was silence in the meeting, but the message was clear to all in attendance.

This message was followed up with a production worker who had openly attempted to verbally sabotage the lean efforts. Eventually the employee signed up to participate in a lean event, and was later praised at one of the meetings for his valuable input and involvement.

To the credit of several senior managers and other key champions who embraced the concept with zeal and enthusiasm, lean became a great success at Markem. Bottom-line financial indicators improved dramatically in many areas, and over the course of a three-year period, Markem became a success story for lean management advocates.

People familiar with lean know it has been regarded by some as a way to focus on improving process management in manufacturing, but lean concepts are intended for all functions and operations within a company. As a cross-functional discipline, lean is a great example for a first foray into Human Capital Management. While it's primarily based on "process," it is "people" centered and relies on the workforce to drive improvements in process change within the organization.

By the way, there's no reason the individual who leads the charge for lean management has to be a manufacturing expert. Instead, the person needs to be someone who has a desire to continuously improve, has an interest in process management, can be a champion within the organization, and is able to persevere through persistence, and overcome roadblocks...all traits critical for the transition to Human Capital Management.

9) Leaders Must Be Willing to Modify Plans and Make Changes as Needed

The best leaders are those willing to make incremental changes in plans as they survey the strategic landscape. From my perspective, this skill is perhaps one of the most underrated and least common you will find in leadership in any sector. Of course, the very best leaders are those who can forecast changes in their industry. But there are few people like Steve Jobs and we can't expect our leaders to have the unique skill to predict strategic inflection points. What we can expect from our leaders is for them to recognize the opportunities that strategic inflection points present, and to have the foresight to make sweeping or incremental changes as they need to occur. When internal or external factors impact business strategies, organizational goals, and initiatives, it's the responsibility of senior management to recognize these and make the necessary changes. Failure to make these changes may result in goals being mismatched with the strategy they're intended to support.

Leaders need to have the courage to make changes in strategy when required, and they also need to have the fortitude to carry on with faith and endurance.

When a CEO plows ahead with a strategy and organizational goals regardless of obvious or non-obvious influencers, he/she is less likely to make changes in those strategies or goals as time goes on. This is a pretty standard human approach if you think about it. If you're walking down a path and someone tells you it will take 30 minutes to get to the end, when you've already travelled 20 minutes down that path, you might be reluctant to turn around and go back at that point. It's not uncommon for people to travel the full 30 minutes, feeling more at ease knowing for certain that they arrived in the right or wrong place.

Unfortunately, while it may be human nature, this type of thinking doesn't work very well in leadership. In the above example, it would've been better for the leader to change course after 10 minutes rather than stubbornly staying the course. But this might require admitting a mistake.

Admitting mistakes is one of the most difficult things for a CEO to do. More often than not, major mistakes aren't acknowledged until management changes have been made. And usually it's the new management regime pointing out the mistakes of the old management regime, since the new CEO often changes the course set by the former CEO.

In the USA, it's culturally acceptable for managers to admit their mistakes. While the acknowledged mistake is seen as a weakness, it's also considered an endearing quality of the individual who took responsibility for it. Assuming mistakes don't happen too often, ruin the company or cause a public relations nightmare such as an environmental disaster, they're usually forgiven. Nonetheless, in business, it's difficult for a CEO to admit a major mistake. He/she needs to maintain confidence with direct reports and the workforce so admitting big mistakes is a gamble. The loss of credibility could be a challenge to overcome. This may be why leaders who change course in mid-stream have difficulty explaining these decisions, and sometimes don't take the time to communicate a change in direction. Obviously this can be very confusing to the workforce.

When employees are confused, they're not going to be easily aligned, nor are they going to be as motivated and ready to go to extraordinary lengths for their employer. This is the reason why it's so necessary for CEOs to explain changes. The best CEOs aren't worried about their egos. In the USA, they can admit when they make a mistake, and they have enough confidence in their abilities that they can openly communicate the reasons for a change in direction.

In a country like Japan, admitting a mistake is culturally accepted, and it's necessary in some cases in order to save one's honor. In other countries, admitting mistakes openly can be cause for concern. A mistake could be thought of as a fundamental personal flaw in character and leadership. In France, admitting a mistake is less acceptable, as it's more likely to be seen as a weakness of character.

There have been numerous examples in the private and public sector where leaders who make mistakes react according to what is culturally acceptable in their own country. However, regardless of country culture, the point is a leader needs to be strong enough to be willing to change direction. The CEO needs to have the best intentions for the organization, and once it's understood a change is needed, it should be communicated and implemented as soon as practical. This should be the case whether or not the mistake is brought about by factors beyond the leadership's control. Failure to communicate a change in direction or mistakes only makes for confusion within the workforce and less confidence and trust in management.

10) Over-Communication is a Key Characteristic of Leadership

Since we've covered Communication in Chapter 15, I'll only make a few comments in this chapter about leadership here. Many HCIs take months to complete, and involve teams of employees, and in some cases the whole workforce. They're very complex and challenging. For this reason it's essential for leaders to make communication a priority and keep employees up-to-date.

The characteristics of good leadership typically include over-communication. I've heard employees complain of too many meetings or too many memos, but I've never heard employees complain of too many direct communications from

top management. Employees are energized when they hear from CEOs and other senior leaders. It gives them a direct line to the top. These types of communications provide motivation and serve to keep the momentum going on a project, especially when it needs a boost.

Communications need to happen as progress occurs. Waiting too long to provide updates can serve to discredit the senior manager. The same holds true for communicating good news and bad news. It's important to be able to communicate both, and this may require a change the workforce needs to hear. The best leaders and CEOs understand good communication is part of their job. It's part of the job description, not an extra skill to be delegated to someone else. There are times when the CEO should delegate to others, but the chief needs to be careful not to over-delegate the communication role.

Chapter 17
Can HR Evolve to Human Capital Management?

Much has been written about how HR has changed over the past ten to fifteen years. In particular, Dave Ulrich and Wayne Brockbank, academic experts in Human Resources for many years and teaching at the University of Michigan, have been champions of the HR function. Separately and together, they've written about HR's transformation in several books and articles. In the 2005 collaboration titled *"The HR Value Proposition,"* they discussed HR work being divided into two categories: transactional activities and strategic transformational activities. In this publication, and others, they've written about the importance of HR professionals needing to be managers of culture and change.

Edward Lawler, another distinguished academic from the University of Southern California was candid and direct in his article *"All About Effectiveness,"* published in Human Resource Executive magazine in November 2005. In this article, Lawler argues that HR must move forward and face the opportunities and challenges to be successful in a global business environment. For the transformational issues, Lawler says for HR to be credible, it *"needs to understand organizational design, organization change and strategy."* [28]

He also matter-of-factly predicted that HR departments not capable of making the transition to being "organizationally effective" will disappear and be outsourced. His prediction has been partially accurate, as many large companies have in fact outsourced their transactional issues. However, outsourcing strategic transformational activities isn't easily accomplished. External vendors don't have access to the internal knowledge of the business required to understand the organization sufficiently. As such, there's an opportunity for Human Resource people inside the company to make a strategic difference in an organization.

It's been several years since these well-respected HR experts have laid down the gauntlet for the HR profession. So the question is, "Has the profession changed measurably during this period of time?"

Without a doubt, the HR discipline has become more professional during this period. The Society of Human Resource Management (SHRM) has grown substantially and it has become standard practice for professionals to take courses and tests to formalize their credentials. But have the majority of HR practitioners advanced measurably in their ability to lead Human Capital transformations or are they still focused on accomplishing tactical actions to support the rest of the organization?

Based on the numerous discussions I've had with HR professionals in networking groups, seminars, conferences, and other exchanges, it's my view that the HR function in general still has stairs to climb in becoming a strategic business partner capable of leading HCIs.

Ulrich, Brockbank, and Lawler have all advocated the reorganization of HR as an important step so transactional services can be efficiently provided while transformational activities can be managed more directly by HR "business partners." This has been a good step in the right direction for companies large enough to be able to make this change. It's not enough though. HR's knowledge, skills, and abilities (KSA's) and overall business contribution needs to be upgraded in order to make the transition to Human Capital Management. Learning how to become change managers is as easy as attending a 3-day seminar, but having the capability to go back to the office and become the company's change agent is another story.

Human Capital Skills Requirements for HR Professionals

So what skills are required for HR professionals to develop into Human Capital Management professionals?

My first piece of advice is for HR people to take stock of their situation and be honest with themselves about their role and contribution to the organization. For those HR people who are not yet practicing at the Human Capital Management level, they should seriously research and review the books and articles already mentioned in this book, as well as the following books listed below. These are a few of the kinds of resources that offer a comprehensive view of Human Capital Management:

- *"Strategic Human Capital Management: Creating Value through People,"* Jon Ingham, 2007

- *"Beyond HR: The New Science of Human Capital,"* John W. Boudreau and Peter M. Ramstad, 2007

- *"Roadmap to Strategic HR: Turning a Great Idea into a Business Reality,"* Ralph Christensen, 2006

Based on my 30+ years of HR management experience, I would also offer the following practical suggestions to those entrusted with or bold enough to move up the value chain from Human Resources to Human Capital Management:

1) You must **know the internal workings of your business**, like who does what and how each function interrelates with other functions? What is the process flow of the business? Understanding the internal workings of the organization allows for a better understanding of the jobs being performed, and how each element of the organization adds value to the business. It puts the Human Capital person on par with his/her functional counterparts in discussing such topics as organizational design, position requirements and the like. This can be achieved by job shadowing, taking courses in other functional disciplines, participating in cross-functional projects ("lean" projects are excellent opportunities, where cross-functional teams are assembled to

improve a process within an organizational function), and participating in orientation meetings other functions are willing to provide.

2) You must **learn how value is derived for the customer**, and learn about what's going on in the industry and competitive environment. In most instances, there's a significant difference in the contribution of what non-HR executives bring to business strategy meetings versus the limited value HR usually brings. In those cases where I've visited customers, attended trade shows or other industry events, and taken the time to understand the nuances of how our products worked, it has been easier for me to participate as a peer in making contributions to strategic and operational decisions. This requires understanding how your company and products provide real value to your customers, and in business-to-business relationships, it goes farther by understanding what value your customers are offering to their customers. Human Capital managers are active participants, not just observers in dealing with business strategy and operational matters.

3) **Becoming an expert in the management of change and management of culture, and understanding how they relate to one another** is a critical element for making the upgrade to Human Capital Management. Learning about these topics is the easy part as there's plenty of literature and seminars available to understand what's required and how to do it. It's more challenging to understand what types of changes are needed, and what the best solutions are to meet those challenges. More specifically:

• **Determine what types of changes need to be advocated.** The CEO or another senior level manager often articulates the need for change. The Human Capital manager needs to have the capability to identify when a significant change effort is needed, and not when it's already obvious as dictated or directed by the CEO. Just as important, the Human Capital manager needs to have the capability to convince other senior managers, including the CEO, of the need for change.

- **Assessing the "culture-change management" relationship is critical**. What do I mean by this? Where a change initiative is required in a healthy organization, one must carefully evaluate the change intervention approaches needed while protecting the key elements of the culture. For example, a company having a strong paternalistic relationship with its employees in a nurturing culture will need to carefully review how it wants to introduce a "performance culture" change initiative. Likewise, the urgency of the change will impact the kind of change intervention or culture change required. Understanding the relationship between the culture of the company and the change effort required is crucial, just as it's crucial for the Human Capital manager to be able to articulate the company's culture. In many companies I've observed, the culture isn't written or it's not written clearly enough to be well understood by the workforce. I recommend that the Human Capital manager should take the lead in articulating the company culture, gain senior management buy-in, and then share it with the workforce. There may be aspects of the culture needing to be changed though. When the Human Capital manager takes the time to study the cultural characteristics, he/she will be in a position to separate those traits needing to be enhanced from those needing to be changed.

4) While the execution of HR management is typically limited to a functional responsibility, **the primary focus of the Human Capital manager is the welfare of the business and the company.** Unlike many HR practitioners, I don't believe it's HR's role to be an "employee advocate." The Human Capital manager is first and foremost a business leader and company advocate. This means he or she should be looking after the interests of the company. However, this postulation acknowledges the Human Capital manager as an intelligent person who understands how to motivate people and believes in the Golden Rule ("treat others the way you would like to be treated yourself") as a key principle of business (and life). With this in mind, the Human Capital manager understands how to balance the role in the company-employee continuum. The Human Capital manager looks at

business decisions objectively seeking to achieve optimal business results, taking into account how human capital decisions will impact business results. The Human Capital manager is different than the HR employee advocate, who by definition is impartial as viewed by his/her peers in the management team. Sincere development of this "company advocate" approach is an important factor in being viewed as an objective and credible player at the senior management table.

5) **Leadership and management are different skills, but both are required for successful Human Capital**. Just as good HR is a prerequisite to Human Capital, in my opinion, good management is a prerequisite to leadership. It's well understood that management and leadership are two different skills, and many would agree an individual could be a good leader without being a good manager. Similarly, an individual could be a good manager without being a good leader. I'd agree one can be a good leader without being a good manager, but to be an effective Human Capital leader, management skills are necessary. The reason for this is simple. Human Capital leaders are engaged in topics on the peripheral of and outside the HR function. They provide guidance and direction, sometimes challenging managers of other business functions in areas not typically HR's domain. In order to have credibility to play this role, HR's house needs to be in order. This requires good management skills to ensure tactical HR functions such as recruitment, compensation, training, and other daily operations are being performed exceptionally well. Without good HR operations in place, the Human Capital leader loses credibility and must go back to HR management, taking time away from strategic matters.

6) Human Capital managers have the vision and capability to create strategy, linking functional goals to organizational goals, and developing project plans to achieve those goals. In other words, **Human Capital leaders have skills to develop and execute the strategy**. I've seen good managers who couldn't make the jump from "Manager" to "Director" or "VP"

because they didn't have the ability to turn their knowledge and skills into a comprehensive skills set allowing them to see the bigger picture. Connecting the dots in any business environment is an essential element of growing. Many young professionals are awed by the insights and decisions of their superiors. Most of the time, these superiors aren't any smarter than their subordinates, but they have time and experience on their side. Mid-level and senior level managers should continually be able to enhance and increase their ability to grow in the depth and breadth of their business knowledge or they will ultimately plateau in the organization.

7) Further, the **Human Capital manager must have skills as a Project Manager**, understanding different techniques to building projects, assembling and launching project teams, and implementing the project itself. Anyone who has managed a project successfully understands company culture is an important element of driving a project. The way the project is developed and launched in a company is usually influenced by the company culture, and project management techniques are excellent vehicles by which to influence the company culture.

8) **One of the most critical skills Human Capital managers have is the ability to look at their business from a "system" point of view.** The Human Capital manager has the ability to understand the elements included in the system, and how they relate to one another. More importantly, the Human Capital manager has the insight and business acumen to know which levers to pull or utilize appropriately within the system to obtain the intended outcome. Human Capital managers understand alignment can be most effectively established when all the elements of the system are operating in tandem. They also understand goals can be reached with less need for corrections later in the game when all the elements of the system are assessed before actions are taken.

The reality is that it takes time and experience to become a Human Capital manager. It becomes easier for people with intelligence and business acumen to more effectively manage or influence the system and its components with depth and breadth of experiences. This "system" view is the foundation upon which the Human Capital manager relies to drive business strategy and goals, and as such, it's the blueprint for human capital organizational initiatives.

Making the Change From HR to Human Capital: Is Your Organization Ready?

From my point of view, "Human Capital is to Human Resources," what "Human Resources was to Personnel" many years ago. The transformation of "Personnel" to "Human Resources" was more than renaming a function. With the change in name came a change in the roles and responsibilities of those performing work on the people side of the business. The same is true today with respect to moving up the value chain from HR to Human Capital Management.

Today there is a significant difference in the contribution level between the most advanced HR practitioners and the rest of the pack. Those teams at the top, the crème-de-la-crème link their strategy, goals, and activities to the overall business strategy to drive organizational initiatives. These companies are performing Human Capital Management. For others, HR is still in the business of managing programs and activities to support other functions within the company or in providing HR services. As mentioned earlier, this is often the case because HR may not have the skills or resources to do the job. It may also be that senior leaders don't see the strategic value HR can bring to the table.

Figure 18 on the next page illustrates the big picture of "bringing value to the people function." There are many people still providing basic essential "personnel" services to the organization, but the added value is greatest where the practice of Human Capital Management resides.

Figure 18

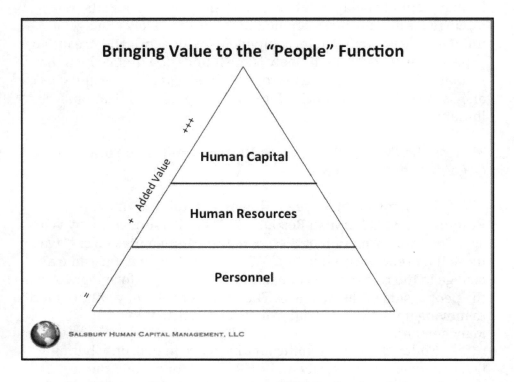

For years, a large percentage of HR professionals have been overly sensitive about not "having a seat at the table," a reference to not being considered an integral member of the senior management team. This has been a "catch-22" for HR in many companies as CEOs and other business leaders didn't understand what HR was capable of achieving or didn't view HR's "non-value added role" as having the same level of importance as other key business functions. In some cases, HR reports to the CFO due to the company's small size, and in other cases, the HR function reports to the CFO regardless of the company's size. This situation only reinforces mediocre HR capabilities as some of the best HR professionals have joined other companies where there's a strong commitment to HR or where there's a CEO who understands HR can bring strategic added value. The inability to play an important senior management role has become a self-fulfilling prophecy in many organizations where the HR incumbent is not invited to participate in strategic activities.

For many HR professionals, the inability to obtain a "seat at the table" is a result of not understanding the business and/or the lack of ability to apply appropriate human capital solutions to problems and needs. On the other hand, those HR leaders who have been successful in operating within the senior management team have been successful in understanding how to apply HR solutions to business needs.

Going forward, for companies who choose to operate as Human Capital Management organizations, it's no longer an option for HR people to be incapable of practicing Human Capital Management. For a company to be successful implementing Human Capital Management, the HR organization must have the capability to make the transition too. For this to happen, there are three critical prerequisites that need to be put in place:

1) The commitment of the CEO and the requirement of a senior HR leader with suitable capabilities is a prerequisite to Human Capital Management.

2) Additionally, it's imperative in making the transition from HR to Human Capital Management, the Human Resource management operations must be well established and functioning satisfactorily. This means HR functions such as payroll, recruiting and staffing, as well as training programs and other basic HR roles and services must already be operating effectively and efficiently.

3) Finally, the organization must be ready for HR to make the transition to Human Capital Management.

The following story is provided to illustrate my point.

Human Cattle or Human Capital?

I'll never forget the reaction of one of my business colleagues the first time I suggested that we rebrand our internal "Human Resources" department to "Human Capital." "You mean, human cattle!" he grinned, as if it was obvious "human capital" was a negative reference showing a lack of respect for HR as well as the people of the company. It wasn't a surprise to me that he had this reaction because the word "capital" equates to "money," and by putting "human" in front of the word "capital" he interpreted it as saying this was a way of devaluing people.

I decided to push this conversation a little further to explore his reaction more deeply and asked him to elaborate. He responded by saying, "The term 'Human Resources' is more respectful of the workforce, and equating people to capital sends a direct message that we employ people for the sole purpose to make money!" He went on to say that while it was true we were in the business to make profits, "Human Capital" was too strong a phrase, and our workforce would not view this name change in a positive way.

I thought carefully about my colleague's response as objectively as possible, but in doing so, I actually became more convinced to remake the HR organization into a "Human Capital" team capable of delivering Human Capital Management. I thought this was the right thing to do because I was convinced there was a significant difference between what Human Capital could provide in added value at that point in our company's life cycle. Additionally, while I understood that Human Capital Management is bigger than HR, I believed there should be a direct correlation between how we characterize or talk about our people, and what we call the department charged with the responsibility to manage our people programs. Most importantly, I wanted our employees to know that they were the difference in our success, and yes, "we did employ people for the primary purpose to make money." For us to be successful in achieving our goals and profits, our employees needed to understand how critical their actions were to the company.

It's true...for-profit companies are in the business to make money. Very few companies today are in the business to "employ people." Companies operating in a capitalist society shouldn't have to apologize for this approach. Even those companies who say in their values statements "people are our number one asset," often downsize or right-size (whichever term you prefer) when the choice needs to be made between losing money and keeping people on the payroll.

Making the Change to Human Capital: The Markem-Imaje Merger

Despite my colleague's reaction, I was convinced it was indeed the time to make the transition to "Human Capital." This decision would benefit the company. At the time, I was working on the merger between Markem and Imaje. The combination of these two companies would be powerful if the merger was done properly. The good news was this wasn't a merger requiring massive expense cuts or headcount reductions as the two companies complemented each other very well. The geographic footprints and product portfolios were complementary. The merger would reduce gaps improving our global market presence and increasing our product range. This wasn't a merger about consolidating market share. It was a merger about combining market share, and then taking steps to leverage the strengths of the combination so that there could be added value and market share gains.

As noted in Chapter 7 on company culture, Markem and Imaje had positive aspects that could be commonly leveraged. Each had similar core values, and one of these was "reliability." Customers saw Imaje as a company with broad geographic reach and strong local service capabilities, and Markem was a well-recognized company for its trustworthy and reliable employees. Markem employees would do what was right for the customer, even at its own expense at times. With these two companies combined, this "reliability" value had the potential to reflect the company's human capital capabilities to a greater extent than either company could do on its own.

As the merger of Markem-Imaje was being prepared, the Marketing department was hard at work building it's messaging so that our combined value could be developed into a competitive advantage. In order for the merger to be successful, it was equally important for our internal view to be consistent with the view of our customers. Otherwise, we would be selling something to our customers and to our employees we couldn't deliver on.

We were a global company with groups of employees located in more than 50 countries around the world – and this translated to "close to our customers." "Reliability" was woven into our marketing theme as well, and the overall brand made it clear that it was our people who made the company special. Doing business with Markem-Imaje was the right thing to do because it was our people who could be depended on and trusted to deliver what our customers needed.

To reinforce this message internally, we told our employees rather than take a fast approach to standardize salaries and benefits, we would take up to a year to review our compensation and benefits programs and not make hasty decisions leaving any one group of employees feeling like they were being treated unfairly. This also gave us the time we needed to fully evaluate our compensation and benefits programs around the world, rather than make quick changes that might cause morale problems.

At the same time, we told our workforce we wouldn't have layoffs or job eliminations, other than mid-level and upper management positions where we only needed one person for a job where there were two. These actions enabled the commercial functions of the organization to focus on customers, instead of having to deal with internal issues. All these actions as well as others put the primary focus on ensuring to the best of our ability, the merger would take place seamlessly and transparently to our customers. This approach added credibility to our messaging both internally and externally. While we realized customers would only buy quality products delivered on a timely basis, we knew our position of strength came from our human capital....our people.

Our main competitor was Videojet, owned and operated by Danaher Corporation, a very successful and well-respected conglomerate headquartered in Chicago. Danaher has a broad range of businesses, and is an aggressive company with a track record of success. It's well-known by its competitors for its Danaher Business Systems, a formalized and systematic approach relying mainly on process management to becoming more efficient, thereby enabling the company to reduce costs and improve its position on pricing and profit margins.

While Videojet's advantage, as perceived by us, was primarily its ability to achieve efficiencies, Markem-Imaje was looking to position itself as the company whose advantage was its people. We believed we could also achieve efficiencies using process management as well as other state-of-the-art tools, but the merger of Markem and Imaje was the perfect opportunity to mobilize our workforce as our differentiator.

I knew that a name change from HR to Human Capital simply to rebrand our department's reputation wasn't a good idea in and of itself. The underlying reason for making this change had to do with leveraging the roles and responsibilities we performed in a way to bring greater value to the company. This change had to fit with our strategy, and it had to come with a compelling organizational initiative that would logically make sense to the organization. The decision to brand and leverage our people as the strength behind our company was the compelling reason to make the change to Human Capital.

Attaining Critical Buy-in was Needed Upfront

I brought the idea of Human Capital to Omar Kerbage, then-President & CEO of Dover's Product Identification Group of which Markem-Imaje was a key component. Omar was a unique individual who seemed to have the Midas touch, as he had a career history of taking mediocre or under-performing companies and turning them into winners. A French citizen of Lebanese descent, and an engineer by training, he had strong sales and marketing savvy. Probably his greatest strength was his ability to link strategy and tactics. He was also profoundly practical, which enabled him to view a situation with more clarity and pragmatism than most people. And he didn't take long to warm up to ideas he bought into. Like many business leaders, Omar liked to move swiftly.

As I made my elevator speech to Omar regarding the transformation of the company to Human Capital Management, and HR's transition to Human Capital, Omar stopped me and said, "Let's do it!"

But that wasn't all. Immediately, he recognized the responsibility and expectation I was placing on my own function to deliver a service above and beyond what was traditionally expected of Human Resources. During the next hour, we spoke about a number of issues related to making the transition to Human Capital. Omar understood that this decision was linked to our business strategy, and to be successful, it would require an organizational commitment and a number of key actions needing to be put in place as preliminary steps.

First, we needed to refine and improve our definition and explanation of what Human Capital Management was intended to be. This was necessary for us to explain from the point of view of the employees as they thought about what was required of them. A central part of this communication would be a convincing and energizing business rationale.

Likewise, we would need to communicate this idea to the Executive Committee, a term we used to refer to the senior management team of the company. Omar and I agreed it was my responsibility to provide the communication to the senior management team and answer any questions they had regarding this change, such as what it meant for the organization, what they could expect in changes from the new Human Capital team, and so on. Omar's role in communicating to the Executive Committee was to introduce and support the topic at our Executive Committee meeting, and he did so convincingly with a brief lead-in to the topic so the other executives were aware he supported the concept. This was important to show the team that this wasn't an open forum for debate, but rather this communication was the first step in the implementation process. Regardless of his support, Omar and I both understood it was my responsibility to respond to valid questions or issues raised by my peers in a professional, appropriate, and satisfactory manner. It was also my responsibility to reflect on any pertinent points brought up by my colleagues where I had perhaps overlooked something or where an improvement could be made.

Beyond the Executive Committee, I needed to then communicate the new Human Capital theme to the HR department employees. Obviously, the HR team needed to hear about the change to Human Capital directly from me, rather than through an organizational announcement or the company grapevine, so my next step was to build a presentation to share with them. Like many new initiatives, the communication needed to have enough detail and definition for the HR team to understand it, but not too much preliminary detail to delay it from being acted on. This was also an opportunity for the team to participate in helping shape the definition.

My initial communication with HR was shared informally with the key HR directors in the different geographic regions of the world. This allowed them the opportunity to digest the Human Capital concept, and it further gave them the opportunity to provide feedback and participate in shaping the message to be delivered to the broader team.

Afterwards, I organized the first worldwide Human Capital meeting of the combined Markem and Imaje HR teams in Barcelona, Spain, and used this forum to present the new Human Capital theme. I invited Omar to attend the meeting, and he opened it with a preview of our business strategy, pointing out the critical need for our company's human capital to play a major role in our transformation. I then proceeded to explain to those in attendance a foundational understanding of what Human Capital Management was all about. Certainly, my description and presentation regarding my image of an upgraded functional role, called Human Capital, seemed like an ambitious goal to them. A strong part of my message included the view of Human Capital in a leadership role within the company, not only as a support organization. I explained that we would need to take a leadership position in driving organizational goals and in particular, our change to Human Capital reflected our company's commitment to proactively leverage our people as our key competitive advantage. I informed them that they would be asked to work towards a higher standard of skills and abilities. I asked for their uncompromising support for the Human Capital concept, as well as a commitment to a higher level of performance and service expectations. Without these, we wouldn't have the capabilities to deliver our promise to the organization, and this would jeopardize the organization's ability to leverage our human capital as a competitive advantage and differentiator.

Following communication to the HR organization, the Marketing organization worked with the new Human Capital team to build a presentation informing the organization of our strategy to leverage the workforce as our primary advantage. And then we made our presentation, including the name change and commitment to Human Capital Management.

To make a long story short, the change from HR to Human Capital wasn't an easy one for the team to make. It didn't happen overnight, and a few people were lost in the process. But over time, the Human Capital organization became more skilled as a key player in the organization. The same could be said for the company's transition to Human Capital Management. There were trying times during the merger and we had our share of doubters. Despite the challenges though, Markem-Imaje succeeded in reaching record level financial results following the merger, while managing people attrition at less than 8%. The company's transformation to Human Capital Management and the motivation of the workforce to be our difference-maker were the keys to our success.

The transformation to Human Capital Management can take place in your organization. It may require any number of changes needing to take place, including an upgrade of skills. If you and your management team are committed to make it happen, there's no stopping you. Mobilizing and motivating your human capital as a competitive advantage and differentiator is the only viable sustainable advantage for the long-term.

This is Human Capital Management.

Final Thoughts

My background is that of an HR practitioner. I started my career in what was then called Personnel and ended my corporate run in what most people now call Human Resources. Frankly, I was never enamored by the part of HR dealing with administration of health care programs, pensions, and the like. I liked designing them, but not administering them. For me, it was always more exciting to connect business strategies to people strategies, and then implement them. For a good part of my corporate career, this was my main focus prior to retiring from Dover Corporation in early 2012.

As you've read, most of the stories and examples in this book come from my own experiences, not from conducting surveys or interviewing executives from other companies. As the years have gone by, I have tried to continue my own learning and growth by keeping current and up-to-date on relevant topics. Some of this personal growth came through training seminars, literature, and conferences, while other development came from networking with other business leaders from inside and outside the companies I worked for.

While I've seen many changes since entering the field of people management over 30 years ago, I've also witnessed a profession that has struggled to find its place in making strategic contributions. While there are many strong HR executives making a significant difference in helping companies achieve their goals, in my opinion, there are a good number of HR executives, managers, and professionals who fall short of adding the kind of contribution required for maximum value to be gained.

It doesn't have to be this way. I wrote this book to help guide people and organizations achieve greatness by mobilizing people as a real asset. Remember, there can only be so many best and brightest people to go around. Don't spend all your time trying to find the best talent. Take the time to focus on the talent you already have in the organization. An organization can be great by leveraging the totality of its workforce, not only by having the best people. There are plenty of examples in life to demonstrate that having the best people is not enough to succeed.

Human Capital Management is about utilization of the workforce as the primary asset of the organization. The actions taken to build an integrated and aligned system of Human Capital Management is the commitment an organization must make if it is to build and maintain a sustainable advantage.

I don't disagree with all of the management gurus who list a variety of skills managers should have to make a strategic contribution, but at the end of the day, it's not the skills themselves that add value. It's the actions taken to support the business foundation, the business strategy, the organizational goals, and the related initiatives to support them.

Whether you're a CEO, HR executive, another senior leader within your organization, an aspiring manager or a student of management, the principles and guidelines provided in this book can be beneficial to you. But in order for this to happen, you must believe to your core that it's the people of your organization who will truly make the difference in your company's future success. For those who have this belief, you must be personally committed to make it happen. Being a leader and pathfinder is not for the timid. It takes courage and conviction to develop Human Capital Management capabilities in an organization.

Are you satisfied that your workforce is providing you with the advantage you need to compete in your markets? If the answer is yes, then congratulations, you are one of the few already practicing the concepts of Human Capital Management. If the answer is no, what's stopping you from being the person to make Human Capital Management a reality in your organization?

A Personal Note

Most of us go through life bound by the definitions and rules others provide in judging our success. This is particularly true in work organizations where others evaluate performance and attitude, and fitting into the company culture is the norm.

As a result of workplace influences and the amount of time we spend in our jobs, it's easy to become influenced by external views of success. Certainly we should play by the rules as we would expect others to, and if you really want something others control, you have to succeed according to their standards.

Too often though, we lose sense of what we truly want and allow others to decide for us what's important to succeed. When this happens, we aren't at peace with ourselves, and more than likely, unhappy. This can prevent one from reaching his/her maximum potential and fulfillment at work and in life.

For those of you who struggle in maintaining a healthy balance between what others define as success for you, and what you define as success for yourself, I offer the following words I wrote for my own family and myself.

I hope you find them beneficial.

Success is

Success is personal. It's experiential.
Your God and you define your level of success, not others...
unless you let them.
Success can be short-lived or long lasting.
It can come early in life or take a lifetime to achieve.
Success is not a title, nor is it passed from one generation to the
next.
There are those who would have you believe success is achieved
through wealth, power or fame.
But one can have all of these and lack success.
For where egos roam, success is absent.
Success comes from effort, diligence, discipline, perseverance,
and fortitude. It is earned honestly and honorably.
Where success is present, so are care, compassion, and humility.
Some will say you have to create your own opportunities to be
successful,
But more likely, success comes from recognizing and acting on
opportunities that pass by, whether obvious or obscure.
So keep your eyes wide open.
Choose your own path. But be true to yourself in deciding what to
pursue.
Then find your own way, and chase your dreams with the utmost
energy and resolve.
For this will bring you true happiness that no one else can
ascribe.
And when the day is done, you will have achieved success through
happiness, knowing you did it the right way, using your God and
your conscience as your guide.

Thanksgiving Day
November 22, 2012
Mark Salsbury

Footnotes

1. Stephen J. Brewer, *Aligning Human Capital in Achieving Business Goals and Strategic Objectives*, (September 2000), 1 http://www.novahrm.wikispaces.com/file/view/Aligning+HR+to+Achieve+Business+Goals.doc

2. Derek Stockley, *Human Capital Concept – definition and explanation* http://derekstockley.com.au/newsletters-05/018-human-capital.html (Jan 2011)

3. Society for Human Resource Management, *Glossary of HR Terms* http://www.shrm.org/templatestools/glossaries/documents/glossary%20of%20human%20resources%20terms.pdf (Dec 2008)

4. Edward L. Gubman, *The Gauntlet is Down*, Journal of Business Strategy, (Nov-Dec 1996)

5. Jim Matthewman and Floriane Matignon of Mercer Human Resource Consulting, *Human Capital Reporting: An Internal Perspective* (Chartered Institute for Personnel and Development, (Jan 2005), 10 http://www.cipd.co.uk/NR/rdonlyres/14186133-F440-47DF92BE-36E5F65B7962/0/humancapguide0105.pdf

6. Robert J. Grossman, *Remodeling HR at Home Depot*, HR Executive, Volume 53, Number 11 (Nov 2008)

7. BusinessDictionary.com, *Definition of "System"* (2013) http://www.businessdictionary.com/definition/system.html#ixzz1ktlBbwNx

8. BusinessDictionary.com, *Definition of "Mission Statement"* (2013)
    http://www.businessdictionary.com/definition/mission-statement.html

9. Business Dictionary, *Definition of "Vision Statement"* (2013)
    http://www.businessdictionary.com/definition/vision-statement.html

10. Patagonia, *Our Reason for Being* (2013)
    http://www.patagonia.com/us/patagonia.go?assetid=2047&ln=140

11. Coca Cola Company, *Mission, Vision & Values* (2013)
    http://www.coca-colacompany.com/our-company/mission-vision-values#TCCC

12. National Park Service, *What are Core Values?* (2013)
    http://www.nps.gov/training/uc/whcv.htm

13. BusinessDictionary.com, *Definition of "Organizational Culture"*
    (2013)
    http://www.businessdictionary.com/definition/organizational- culture.html#ixzz1nOpzXfAg

14. *Markem-Imaje Values* (2008)

15. Rapid Business Intelligence Success, *A Definition to Business Strategy* (2008)
    http://www.rapid-business-intelligence-success.com/definition-of-business-strategy.html

16. Kodak, *Upholding the Kodak Mission (2013)*
    http://www.kodak.com/ek/US/en/Our_Company/Careers_at_Kodak/Why_Join_Kodak/Kodak_Values_and_Mission.htm

17. Society of Human Resource Management, *The SHRM Global Learning System, Module One: Strategic HR Management (SHRM 2009)*, 103-108

18. Search CIO, *Definition of Business Process Management* (BPM) Jan 2011
http://searchio.techtarget.com/definition/business-process-management

19. Markem, *Principles of Markem Redeployment Policy* (2004)

20. Management Study Guide, *Definition of Business Policy* (2008-2013)
http://managementstudyguide.com/business-policy.htm

21. WhatIs.com, *Definition of Policy Based Management* (Jan 2011)
http://whatis.techtarget.com/definition/policy-based-management

22. SuccessFactors, *Definition of Talent Management* (2013)
http://www.successfactors.com/en_us/lp/articles/strategic-talent-management-training.html

23. Society of Human Resource Management, *Glossary of HR Terms* (2013)
http://www.shrm.org/TemplatesTools/Glossaries/HRTerms /Pages/t.aspx

24. Matt Rivera, *The Seamless Workforce, Talent Acquisition: A Definition* (May 2011)
http://blog.yoh.com/2011/05/talent-acquisition-a-definition.html

25. Jac Fitz-Enz and Barbara Davison, *How to Measure Human Resources Management*, Third Edition, (New York: McGraw-Hill, 2002), 211-22

26. Society of Human Resource Management, *Glossary of HR Terms* (2013)
http://www.shrm.org/TemplatesTools/Glossaries/HRTerm/Pages/o.aspx

27. *The Free Dictionary* citing The American Heritage Dictionary of the English Language, Fourth Edition (Houghton Miffin Company, 2009)
http://www.thefreedictionary.com/framework

28. Edward Lawler, *All About Effectiveness*, Human Resource Executive, (Nov 2005)

Mark P. Salsbury is a Human Capital executive with 30+ years of business experience in management and leadership positions in North America, Europe, and Asia. His international executive experience includes three years in Singapore, and three years in Paris, France. Following his retirement from Dover Corporation in 2012, Mark launched Salsbury Human Capital Management, LLC, a management consulting firm specializing in helping organizations gain a competitive advantage through maximizing their human capital potential.

Prior to launching Salsbury Human Capital Management, LLC, Mark served as the Senior Vice President of Human Capital for Dover Corporation's Product Identification Group (PIDG), a one billion dollar company with 4,000+ employees worldwide. In this position, Mark was a primary facilitator for the merger of Markem Corporation and Imaje Corporation into Markem-Imaje, and he had responsibility for executive and organizational development, as well as overseeing human resources management globally.

Previously, he served as Vice President of Human Resources for Markem Corporation, a privately held company with employees in 17 countries around the world and 1,200 employees. Markem was acquired by Dover Corporation in 2006.

Before joining Markem Corporation, Mark served as worldwide HR leader for Schlumberger Limited's high technology group of companies with almost two billion dollars in sales, 22 factories, 10 product centers, and 9,000 employees.

Mark has a BS degree from Utica College of Syracuse University and an MPA specializing in Management from the State University of New York at Albany.

He is certified as a Senior Professional in Human Resources (SPHR), and as a Global Professional in Human Resources (GPHR). He is also a graduate of the University of Michigan's Strategic Human Resources Planning Program.

Mark has and continues to serve as a professional speaker in the USA and abroad on a variety of topics.